A BOOK OF FAVORITE RECIPES

Compiled by

THE LADIES MINISTRIES

of the

PASADENA CHURCH OF GOD

World's Largest Publisher of Personalized Cook Books
Fund Raising Programs and Programs of Service
For Church, School and Civic Organizations
Printed in the United States of America

Pasadena Church of God

7975 Tickneck Road
PASADENA, MD. 21122

Pastor: Glen H. Morris

Office 255-3168
Home 255-8403

SCHEDULE OF WORSHIP SERVICES

SUNDAYS 9:45 A.M. Sunday BIBLE School
10:45 A.M. Morning Worship
(Children's Worship)
6:30 P.M. Praise Service
(Nursery provided for all services)

WEDNESDAYS - (Family Training Hour)

7:00 P.M. A time of Spiritual Growth
And Enrichment for all the Family

BUILDING ON A FIRM Foundation

Favorite Family Recipes

Expression of Appreciation

The Ladies Ministries of the Pasadena Church of God wish to thank all who have helped in the preparation of this cookbook by way of sharing their favorite recipes with us. We hope that everyone has as much fun using it as we have had putting it together for you.

We have endeavored to combine the practical with the unusual in order to provide an outstanding book of favorite foods that will be treasured and enjoyed by all.

My Favorite Recipes

NAME OF RECIPE	PAGE NO.

APPETIZERS
PICKLES • RELISH

New Hints

Use paper cups as handy containers for your "drippings" in the refrigerator as they take up little room and can be thrown away when empty.

To remove burned-on starch from your iron, sprinkle salt on a sheet of waxed paper and slide iron back and forth several times. Then polish it with silver polish until roughness or stain is removed.

Spray garbage sacks with ammonia to prevent dogs from tearing the bags before picked up.

You can clean darkened aluminum pans easily by boiling in them two teaspoons of cream of tartar mixed in a quart of water. Ten minutes will do it.

To dry drip-dry garments faster and with fewer wrinkles, hang garment over the top of a dry cleaner's plastic bag.

When food is too salty add a cut raw potato, then discard the potato once it is boiled.

If the dish is too sweet, add salt. On a main dish you can add a teaspoon of vinegar.

If the food is too sharp, a teaspoon of sugar will soften the taste.

If a main dish or vegetable is too sweet add a teaspoon or two of vinegar.

To pick up slivers of glass, it helps to use a dampened paper towel.

If zippers stick, just run some bar soap over the zipper and the zipper will work fine.

To draw a straighter line, use a knife instead of a pencil.

To prevent your salt shaker from clogging up, keep a few grains of rice inside the shaker.

To remove your child's crayon marks from linoleum or tile, use silver polish.

Most times very hot water will revive your wilted flowers.

Cheese will not dry out if it is wrapped in a cloth dampened with vinegar.

Your new white tennis shoes will last longer if sprayed heavily with starch when you first get them.

To get the corn silk off of corn on the cob, brush downward with a paper towel.

To cut a pie into five equal pieces, first cut a Y in the pie and then two large pieces can be cut in half.

CUCUMBER SANDWICHES — Pam Higdon (Hawaii)

1 (8 oz.) pkg. cream cheese
1/4 c. mayonnaise
1 pkg. Good Seasons Italian dressing mix
petite rye bread (pumpernickel is best!)
sliced cucumber
dill weed

Mix first 3 ingredients with electric mixer. Spread on bread slices. Top with a cucumber slice. Then sprinkle with dill weed.

HOT CRAB SPREAD — Carol Clevenger

1-2 lbs. crabmeat
2 (8 oz.) cream cheese
8 oz. sour cream
4 Tbsp. mayonnaise
1 Tbsp. Worcestershire sauce
1 Tbsp. lemon juice
salt and pepper
Old Bay seasoning

Mix all ingredients (EXCEPT half the cheese), pour into greased 8 1/2 x 11 baking dish. Bake at 350° for 25-30 minutes. Sprinkle with Old Bay and rest of cheese. Return to oven till cheese is melted.

SPINACH BALLS — Linda Laurence

2 (10 oz.) pkgs. frozen spinach
3 c. herb seasoned stuffing
1 large onion, chopped
6 eggs, beaten
3/4 c. butter, melted
1/2 c. Parmesan cheese
2 tsp. pepper
1/2 tsp. thyme
1 1/2 tsp. garlic salt

Cook and drain frozen spinach. Combine spinach with remaining ingredients. Shape into 1/2-inch balls and place on cookie sheet.

Bake at 350° for 10 minutes. May be frozen and reheated.

SOFT SPREAD CHEESE BALL — Linda Laurence

12 oz. bowl soft whipped Wispride Cheddar cheese
2 (8 oz.) cream cheese
1 tsp. garlic salt
1 tsp. minced onion
1 tsp. water

Mix all together with mixer. Put in a bowl lined with waxed paper. Chill 24 hours. Top with nuts or bacon bits.

JALAPENO SQUARES

Linda Laurence

2 eggs
1 large can evaporated milk
1 c. flour
1 lb. Cheddar cheese
1 lb. Monterey Jack cheese
1/2 c. jalapeno peppers

Line a pan with peppers. Grate and mix cheese and cover peppers. Blend eggs, flour and milk in blender and pour over cheese.

Bake at 350° for 40 minutes. If you want to you may chop peppers and fold into the milk mixture.

CHILI CON QUESO

Kris Leonard

1 chopped onion
1 chopped tomato
1 can taco sauce
1 lb. shredded cheese, half Cheddar, half Velveeta

Saute onion and tomato in oil. Melt cheese, add to vegetables. Add taco sauce, mix thoroughly.

Keep heated in chafing dish or fondue pot, thin with milk if necessary. Serve with tortilla chips.

BOURSIN

Debbie Owen

16 oz. cream cheese
8 oz. whipped butter
1/2 tsp. oregano
1/4 tsp. salad herbs
1/4 tsp. pepper
1/4 tsp. majoram
1/4 tsp. thyme
touch of garlic

Mix together, serve on French bread.

SAUSAGE BISCUITS

Kris Leonard

3 c. Bisquick
1 lb. hot sausage
10 oz. sharp Cheddar cheese, grated

Mix sausage and cheese into Bisquick, shape into small balls. Bake at 350° for 10-15 minutes.

SHRIMP MOLD

Kris Leonard

1 can tomato soup
1/4 c. cold water
1 c. Miracle Whip
1 pkg. crab meat
1 c. small shrimp
1/2 c. chopped onion
1/2 c. chopped celery
1/2 c. chopped green peppers
2 pkgs. unflavored gelatin
1 (8 oz.) pkg. cream cheese

Heat soup to boiling, dissolve gelatin in water and add to soup, mix cheese and Miracle Whip, add to soup, beat mixture with beater, add seafood, vegetables, pour into mold; refrigerate.

SHRIMP DIP — **Linda Laurence**

8 oz. pkg. cream cheese
1/2 c. chili sauce
1/2 c. mayonnaise
1/4 c. chopped onion
2 tsp. horseradish
4 1/2 oz. can shrimp

Add softened cream cheese to chili sauce. Gradually add remaining ingredients. Mix well. Add shrimp and chill at least 2 hours.

CUCUMBER SANDWICHES — **Pam Higdon (Hawaii)**

1 (8 oz.) pkg. cream cheese
1/4 c. mayonnaise
1 pkg. Good Seasons Italian dressing mix
petite rye bread (pumpernickel is best!)
sliced cucumber
dill weed

Mix first 3 ingredients with electric mixer. Spread on bread slices. Top with a cucumber slice. Then sprinkle with dill weed.

SHRIMP COCKTAIL DIP — **Paula Scheerer**

1 c. catsup
2 Tbsp. horseradish
small bag small frozen shrimp
soft cream cheese

Rinse frozen shrimp, separate and drain; set aside.

Mix catsup, horseradish and soft cream cheese, then add shrimp. Serve on crackers.

DIRTY DIAPERS — **Paula Scheerer**

1 lb. ground round
8 oz. shredded Cheddar cheese
2 cans crescent rolls

Fry and drain ground round. Salt and pepper to taste. Stir in Cheddar cheese until mixture sticks together. Open up crescent rolls, spoon mixture on them. Fold each roll over the mixture, shaping it to look like a diaper. Place on a greased cookie sheet and bake at 450° for 8-10 minutes or until lightly browned.

TOASTY ONION STICKS

Sharon Kline

1/2 c. onion butter (see below)
12 slices enriched white bread or soft wheat bread

Onion Butter:

1 envelope Lipton onion soup mix
1/2 lb. butter or margarine

Blend. Makes 1 1/4 cups. Refrigerate remainder. Use with baked potatoes or over vegetables. Preheat oven to 375°. Trim crusts from bread. Spread onion butter on bread slices. Cut each slice into 5 strips. Place strips on ungreased baking sheet. Bake 10 minutes or until golden.

Makes about 5 dozen sticks.

WAIKIKI MEATBALLS

Frances Powers

1 1/2 lbs. extra-lean ground beef
2/3 c. Ritz cracker crumbs
1/3 c. minced onion
1 egg
1 1/2 tsp. salt
2 Tbsp. cornstarch
13 1/2 oz. can pineapple tidbits
1/2 c. brown sugar, packed
1/3 c. vinegar
1 Tbsp. soy sauce
1/3 c. chopped green pepper

Mix ground beef, cracker crumbs, minced onion, egg and salt. Shape mixture by rounded tablespoon into balls. Brown and cook meatballs in large skillet, using 1 tablespoon vegetable oil per skillet full. Remove meatballs and drain skillet when finished.

Mix in a bowl the cornstarch and the syrup from the can of pineapple (DO NOT ADD PINEAPPLE BITS YET, ONLY SYRUP); brown sugar; vinegar and soy sauce. Pour into drained skillet. Cook over medium heat, stirring constantly, until mixture thickens and boils. Boil and stir 1 minute.

Add pineapple tidbits and 1/3 cup chopped green pepper. Add meatballs. Heat through and serve in warmer.

TACO DIP — Mary Rowe

2 (8 oz.) pkgs. cream cheese
1 (8 oz.) sour cream
1 pkg. taco seasoning mix (I use mild)
shredded lettuce
chopped tomato
shredded cheese

Cream together and put in shallow dish. Put lettuce, tomato and shredded cheese on top. Serve with tortilla chips.

HOT CHIPPED BEEF DIP — Bobbi Dorsey

16 oz. cream cheese
1 c. sour cream
4 oz. chipped beef, chopped
1 chopped onion
1/2 tsp. pepper

Combine all ingredients and let sit in refrigerator until ready to serve. When ready, put in microwave and cook for a few minutes until warm/hot.

Or put in 350° oven till warm. Serve with crackers or chips.

NUT CHEESE BALL — Mary Parsons

8 oz. sharp Cheddar cheese, shredded
8 oz. shredded Swiss cheese
8 oz. softened cream cheese
2 tsp. Worcestershire sauce
1/2 tsp. paprika
1/2 tsp. garlic salt
1/3 c. chopped nuts

Place Cheddar cheese, Swiss cheese and cream cheese, Worcestershire sauce, paprika and garlic salt in bowl. Beat at medium speed until well blended.

Shape mixture into a ball. Roll ball in chopped nuts. Wrap in waxed paper and refrigerate until serving time. Serve with crackers or raw vegetable sticks.

Yield: 1 (24-ounce) ball.

SAUSAGES SUPREME — Bonnie Carter

1 (10 oz.) jar apricot jelly
3 Tbsp. mustard
1 lb. cooked sausage links, cut into bite-size pieces

Melt jelly in double boiler. Stir in mustard. Mix well. Add sausage pieces. Stir to coat well. Keep warm in a fondue pot. Let folks serve themselves with toothpicks.

HOT CRAB DIP

Becky Marcucci

1/2 lb. (8 oz.) crabmeat
8 oz. softened cream cheese
1/2 c. sour cream
2 Tbsp. salad dressing
1 Tbsp. lemon juice
1 1/4 tsp. Worcestershire sauce
1/2 tsp. dry mustard
pinch garlic salt
1 Tbsp. milk
1 c. grated Cheddar cheese

Remove cartilage from crabmeat. In large bowl, mix cream cheese, sour cream, salad dressing, lemon juice, Worcestershire, mustard and garlic salt until smooth. Add enough milk to make mixture creamy. Add 2 tablespoons grated cheese. Fold in crabmeat.

Pour into greased 1-quart casserole. Top with remaining cheese. Bake at 325° about 30 minutes or until browned on top and mixture is bubbly.

CRAB MOUSSE

Bonnie Carter

8 oz. cream cheese, softened
1 envelope Knox gelatine
3/4 c. finely chopped red onion
1 c. mayonnaise
1 can cream of mushroom soup
1 c. finely chopped celery
8 oz. crab meat
2 Tbsp. lemon juice

Dissolve gelatine in 3 tablespoons cold water. Heat soup to warm and add gelatine. Beat till smooth with electric mixer. Add mayonnaise and lemon juice slowly. Mix in onion, celery and crab. Blend well. Pour into mold sprayed with Pam. Chill overnight. Serve with crackers.

CHEESE BALL

Linda Murphy

1 lb. Velveeta cheese
1 lb. sharp Cheddar cheese
1 (8 oz.) cream cheese
10 drops Worcestershire sauce
1/4 tsp. garlic powder
3/4-1 c. mayonnaise

Mix well in mixer or food processor. Chill, form into ball. Roll in ground walnuts. Serves a lot!

CHEESE FONDUE

Linda Murphy

1/4 c. butter or margarine
1/4 c. flour
1/2 tsp. salt
1/4 tsp. pepper
1/4 tsp. dry mustard
1/4 tsp. Worcestershire sauce
1 1/2 c. milk
2 c. shredded Cheddar cheese (about 8 oz.)

In saucepan, melt butter over low heat. Blend in flour, salt, pepper, dry mustard and Worcestershire sauce. Cook over low heat, stirring until mixture is smooth and bubbly.

Remove from heat; stir in milk. Heat to boiling, stirring constantly. Boil and stir 1 minute. Stir in cheese; heat over low heat, stirring constantly, until cheese melts.

Pour into fondue pot; transfer to source of heat at table. Adjust heat when necessary to keep fondue warm. Spear dippers and swirl in fondue.

Dippers: Hot brown and serve sausages, cut into thirds; hot canned tiny whole potatoes; cherry tomatoes; hot dogs, cut in pieces and browned; toasted English muffins, cut into pieces.

Write your extra recipes here:

Write your extra recipes here:

SOUPS · SALADS
SAUCES · DRESSINGS

THE SOUP POT

* Steak, roast or poultry bones can be frozen until needed for soup stock.

* If the soup or stew is too salty, add cut raw potatoes and discard them once they have cooked and absorbed the salt.

* Instant soup stock will always be on hand if you save the pan juice from cooking meats. Pour liquid into ice cube trays and freeze. Place solid cubes in freezer bags or foil.

* To prevent curdling of the milk or cream in soup add the soup to the milk rather than vice versa. Or add a bit of flour to the milk and beat well before combining.

* Always start cooking bones and meat in cold, salted water.

* The easiest way to skim off fat from soup is to chill until the fat hardens on top of the liquid. If time will not permit this, wrap ice in paper toweling and skim over the top.

THE SALAD BOWL

* To remove the core from a head of lettuce, hit the core end sharply against the counter top or side of sink. Then the core will twist out easily.

* Put salad greens or cole slaw in a metal bowl and place in the freezer for a few minutes.

* Rubbing waxed paper over the inside and outside of a wooden salad bowl will prevent it from becoming sticky.

* If you cut the root end off the onion last you'll shed less tears.

* To prevent soggy salads, place an inverted saucer in the bottom of the salad bowl. The excess dressing will drain under the saucer and keep the greens crisp.

* Lettuce and celery will crisp up faster if you add a few raw slices of potato to the cold water you use to soak them.

SAUCE SUGGESTIONS

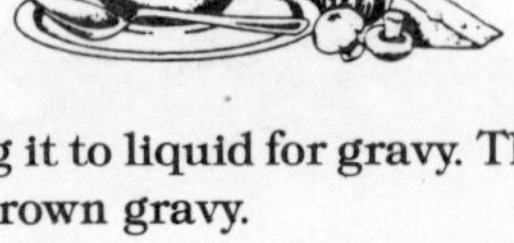

* Make sure that flour is well browned before adding it to liquid for gravy. This will prevent lumpy gravy and also assure a rich brown gravy.

* Placing flour in a custard cup in the oven next to the roast will assure nice brown flour for gravy when the meat is done.

BONAVENTURE HOUSE DRESSING WITH YOGURT AND HERBS
Low-cal

1/2 c. plain non-fat yogurt
1/2 c. reduced-calorie mayonnaise
1 Tbsp. horseradish, drained if watery
1 Tbsp. Dijon mustard*
1 Tbsp. chopped fresh parsley
1 tsp. minced fresh dill
1/4 tsp. celery seeds
1/4-1/2 c. low-fat buttermilk
freshly ground pepper

Combine first 7 ingredients in medium bowl and whisk to blend. Gradually whisk in enough buttermilk to bring dressing to desired consistency. Season with pepper. (Can be prepared 3 days ahead.) Cover and refrigerate.

Makes about 1 1/2 cups; about 20 calories per tablespoon. Also makes a good vegetable dip.

*This is too much mustard for me. You might want to use less or even leave it out.

BEEF-VEGETABLE SOUP

Sherry Heward

1 lb. beef round or stew meat
1 Tbsp. oil
1 small onion, minced
1 tsp. salt
1/8 tsp. black pepper
1/4 c. barley
1 (10 1/2 oz.) can beef broth
2 cans water
1 (8 1/2 oz.) can tomatoes
2 medium carrots, peeled, diced
1 zucchini, sliced

1. Cut beef into small 1/2-inch wide strips. In heavy 3-quart saucepan, brown lightly in hot oil.
2. Add onion. Saute 3 to 4 minutes.
3. Add salt, black pepper, barley, broth, water and tomatoes. Bring to a boil. Cover and simmer 30 minutes.
4. Add carrots and zucchini. Bring to a boil again. Simmer 15 to 20 minutes longer or until vegetables and barley are tender.
5. Serve in bowl with cheese croutons.

JIFFY MINESTRONE SOUP

Bobbi Dorsey

4 c. coarsely chopped cabbage (1/2 medium-size head)
1 medium onion, chopped
1/4 c. chopped parsley
2 cloves garlic, chopped
1 tsp. each: salt and oregano
1/4 tsp. pepper
3 Tbsp. oil
5 c. beef broth
1 (16 oz.) can tomatoes or 2 c. fresh
1/4 lb. broken spaghetti
1 (16 oz.) can red kidney beans

In Dutch oven over medium heat, saute cabbage, onion, parsley, garlic and pepper in oil, stirring often, 5 minutes or until cabbage is crisp-tender.

Add broth and tomatoes; bring to a boil. Stir in spaghetti and beans. Cook, stirring occasionally, 10 minutes or until spaghetti is done.

Makes 8 servings. Per serving: 200 calories, 15 mg chol., 842 mg sodium, 6 g fat.

MEATBALL STEW

Mary Parsons

1 lb. ground beef
1/4 c. uncooked rice
1/2 tsp. garlic powder
1/4 c. Parmesan cheese
salt
2 (15 oz.) cans tomato sauce
1 Tbsp. vegetable oil
1 c. diced onion
1 c. sliced celery
1 c. sliced carrots
2 lbs. chopped potatoes
(water)

Combine ground beef, rice, garlic powder, Parmesan cheese and 1 teaspoon salt. Form mixture into approximately 20 meatballs. Brown meatballs with vegetable oil in Dutch oven. Drain fat.

Add tomato sauce and remaining ingredients. Cover, simmer 30 minutes or until vegetables are done. Add water to desired consistency.

Yield: 6-8 servings.

FRENCH POTATO SALAD

Freida Marsh

6 potatoes, cooked
3 hard-boiled eggs
1 diced cucumber
1/4 tsp. paprika
1/4 c. French dressing
1 chopped onion
1 c. chopped celery
1 1/2 tsp. salt
1 c. grated carrot
mayonnaise

Combine ingredients except dressing. Chill and marinate

in French dressing for 6 hours.

Before serving add mayonnaise and mix. Makes 8 servings.

GREEN PEA CASSEROLE

Paula Scheerer

1 box frozen peas
1 can mushrooms
1 small can pimentos
1 can tomato soup
1/2 c. chili sauce
1 tsp. Worcestershire
bread crumbs
1 1/2 c. mushroom soup
  diluted with 1/2 c. milk
1 c. grated cheese
1 chopped green pepper
6 hard-boiled eggs
1 c. chopped celery
butter

Mix everything together except mushroom soup and eggs and bread crumbs.

Put in casserole in layers covering each with mushroom soup and sliced eggs. Cover with bread crumbs. Dot with butter and bake in 350° oven for about an hour.

Serves 6.

BROCCOLI SALAD

Misty Frye

1 large bunch broccoli,
  finely chopped
8 strips bacon, fried crisp
  and crumbled
1/2 c. sugar
2 Tbsp. vinegar
1/2 c. raisins
1 medium red onion, chopped
1/2 c. pecans, chopped
1 c. salad dressing
1 tsp. salt

Blend salad dressing, vinegar and sugar. Combine with all other ingredients. Refrigerate 1 hour and serve.

PASTA SALAD

Linda Murphy

1 lb. twist noodles (spinach,
  tomato and regular)
1/4 lb. cooked ham, cut
  into pieces
chopped green pepper
sliced green onions
chopped tomatoes
shredded Cheddar cheese
1 (8 oz.) Italian dressing

Cook noodles, rinse in cold water. Mix noodles with other ingredients and then add dressing and mix well. Refrigerate several hours or overnight before serving.

ENGLISH POTATO SALAD

Kathrenai P. Letson

2 or 3 lbs. potatoes
3 celery sticks plus parsley
salt and pepper to taste
1 large onion or 4 scallions (use the green part)
2 hot peppers, save the juice for later
1 c. Miracle Whip
2 Tbsp. hot pepper juice

Boil potatoes, cool. Cut up in small. Set aside. Chop onions, parsley, celery, hot peppers, very fine chopping. Mix with Miracle Whip. Pour over potatoes and mix well. Leave overnight in refrigerator.

Very good potato salad.

PASTA SALAD

Laurie Downey

1 (16 oz.) box spiral noodles
1 large bottle Italian salad dressing
1 small can Parmesan cheese
1 jar Salad Supreme (found in spice aisle)
1 c. diced cucumbers
1 c. diced tomatoes

Cook noodles per package directions, drain well. Toss remaining ingredients with noodles. Can be served warm or cold.

TUNA SALAD

Sherry Heward

3 eggs, hard cooked
1 1/2 cans (4 1/2 oz.) tuna
3/4 c. celery, sliced
2 green onions, minced
1/2 c. mayonnaise
1 Tbsp. lemon juice
salt and pepper to taste

1. Chop eggs.
2. Mix eggs with tuna, celery, onion, mayonnaise, lemon juice, salt and pepper. Toss lightly. Chill 2 hours or more.

PEA SALAD

Paula Scheerer

small box frozen peas
2 Tbsp. mayonnaise
2 stalks celery, chopped
1 small onion, chopped
1 Tbsp. celery seed

Rinse peas in cold water, separate and drain. Mix with other ingredients and chill.

PENNSYLVANIA DUTCH MACARONI SALAD

Serves 8. **Debbie Caldwell**

Cook in saucepan:

1 1/2 c. sugar
1/4 c. flour
1/3 c. vinegar
1 1/2 c. water
1 tsp. salt

Cook these ingredients till creamy; set aside to cool. Cook 1/2-3/4 box macaroni noodles, drain. Prepare:

1 c. chopped celery (optional)
1/2 chopped medium onion
5 hard-boiled eggs, chopped
1 large grated carrot
1 c. mayonnaise
1/4 c. mustard

Mix these ingredients in large bowl with cooled noodles and cooked sauce. Mix well. Top with a sprinkle of paprika.

3 BEAN SALAD

Debbie Caldwell

1 1/2 lbs. ground beef
3/4 lb. bacon, cut into small pieces, fry and drain
1 c. chopped onions
1 large can pork and beans
1 large can kidney beans, drained
1 large can butter beans, drained
2 c. ketchup
1/2 c. brown sugar
6 tsp. white vinegar
2 tsp. Colgin hickory liquid smoke
1 tsp. salt
1/2 tsp. pepper

Mix all ingredients together.

1. Brown onion and beef, drain.
2. Cook 4 to 6 hours on medium in a slow cooker.

SPAGHETTI SALAD

Mrs. Sam Gladwin

1 lb. spaghetti
1 bottle Italian dressing
1/2 bottle Salad Supreme
1 cucumber, chopped
1 tomato, chopped
1 green pepper, chopped
1 bunch green onions, chopped
mushrooms (optional)

Mix all ingredients well and chill at least 1 hour before serving.

Great for a picnic, potluck dinner or serving a large crowd.

LINGUINI SALAD

Betty Adelung

1 lb. linguini, cooked (break linguini in half before cooking)
1 large bottle Caesar's salad dressing
1 bottle Salad Supreme (McCormick spice)
2 large tomatoes, sliced and quartered
2 cucumbers, sliced and quartered
1 large onion, diced

Cook and drain linguini. Add Salad Supreme and mix thoroughly. Add all other ingredients and mix. Refrigerate until chilled.

SUMMER SALAD

Linda Murphy

cucumber
tomatoes
onion
salt
pepper
sour cream

Cut vegetables into bite-size pieces. Right before serving salt and pepper to taste. Add sour cream to coat vegetables.

TACO SALAD

Linda Laurence

2 medium tomatoes
1 large lettuce
1 lb. ground beef
1 (16 oz.) bag mild Cheddar cheese, grated
1 large bag plain corn chips
1 large onion
1 (16 oz.) bottle Kraft Catalina dressing

Brown ground beef in Old Bay seasoning, garlic salt and grated Parmesan cheese.

First chop tomatoes, then add cheese, lettuce, meat, onion. Chill for 1 hour.

Just before serving add chips (crushed) and dressing.

KIDNEY BEAN AND TUNA SALAD

Bobbi Dorsey

15 1/2 oz. can no-salt kidney beans, drained
6 1/2 oz. can water packed tuna, drained
2 Tbsp. plain low-fat yogurt
1/2 c. chopped celery
1/2 c. chopped green pepper
3 Tbsp. pickle relish or 1 Tbsp. minced onion
1/4 tsp. dill
1/2 tsp. black pepper

Mix all ingredients and chill. Serves 4 at 150 calories,

4 grams fiber and 3 grams fat per 3/4 cup serving.

Write your extra recipes here:

Write your extra recipes here:

MAIN DISHES
MEAT • POULTRY
SEA FOOD

MEAT, SEAFOOD AND POULTRY NOTES

* Baking fish on a bed of celery and onions will add to the taste as well as keep the fish from sticking.

* Coating will adhere to chicken better if it has been chilled for an hour before cooking.

* Sprinkle salt in the frying pan before adding meat and there will be less grease splattered.

* For a juicier burger rub both sides with cold water before grilling.

* Place cold water and cornstarch or flour in a jar with tight lid. Shake the jar until liquid is well mixed and lumps are gone. Then slowly add this mixture to pan drippings and stir while bringing gravy to a boil.

* Always roast poultry breast side down so the white meat will not dry out. Turn the bird for the last portion of cooking so that it will brown well.

* Rubbing poultry with salt and lemon juice will lessen any unpleasant odor.

* Bacon won't stick together if the package is rolled into a tube and secured before refrigerating.

* For a ham that's too salty, drain liquid off when it's half finished baking and add 10 oz. of ginger ale to the meat and bake until done.

* Unwaxed dental floss is good for trussing poultry because it will not burn.

* If gravy is too greasy, a bit of baking soda can be added without affecting the taste of the gravy.

* Soak bacon in cold water for a few minutes before frying and it won't curl as much as usual.

* A dash of lemon juice and milk added to the liquid used to cook white fish will make the flesh white.

* Chicken marinated in milk or buttermilk for several hours in the refrigerator will be more tender.

* Pour pan drippings into a tall jar. The grease will rise to the top in minutes and can be removed for grease free gravy.

* Meat loaf won't crack when baking if it's rubbed with cold water before going in the oven.

* Adding cold water to the bottom of the broiling pan before cooking meat helps absorb smoke and grease and makes clean up easier.

MAIN DISHES - MEAT, SEAFOOD AND POULTRY

TEXAS HASH

Kathy Letson

1 lb. ground beef
1 medium onion
1/2 green pepper
1/3 c. rice
1 (No. 2) can tomatoes
salt and pepper (black) and chili powder (to taste)

Use 1 tablespoon of oil in skillet, cut up onion, bell pepper and ground beef, brown all together. Add tomatoes, rice, salt, pepper and chili powder. Simmer a few minutes.

Pour into a baking dish, cover and bake in 375° oven for 45 minutes.

STUFFED PEPPERS, ITALIAN STYLE

Stuffing:

1 lb. hamburger
3-4 sweet Italian sausages, out of casing
1 1/2 c. Parmesan cheese
2 pkgs. frozen spinach, thawed
2-3 eggs
1 1/2 tsp. Italian seasoning
salt/pepper
bread crumbs, if necessary

Combine all of above. Stuff into raw peppers and bake at 350° about 45 minutes. Then turn upside down on paper towel to drain off grease before serving.

HAM STROGANOFF

Aunt Oleta

Serves 4.

2 c. ham strips
1/2 c. chopped onion
2 Tbsp. butter
1 (4 oz.) can mushrooms
1 can mushroom soup
1 (8 oz.) carton sour cream
cooked egg noodles

Saute ham, onion, butter and mushrooms. Add soup and heat through. Gently add sour cream (if it boils it will separate). Serve over noodles.

GREEN PEPPER STEAK

Bonnie Swecker

Cook these first 4 ingredients for 30 to 40 minutes:

1 lb. beef chuck or round (fat trimmed)
1/4 c. soy sauce
1 clove garlic
1 1/2 grated ginger or 1/2 tsp. ground
1/4 c. salad oil
1 c. green onions, sliced thin
1 c. green peppers, cut into 1-inch squares
2 stalks celery, thinly sliced
1 Tbsp. cornstarch
1 c. water
2 tomatoes, cut into wedges

With sharp knife cut beef across grain into thin strips 1/8-inch thick.

Combine soy sauce, garlic, ginger while preparing vegetables. Heat oil in large frying pan. Add beef and toss over high heat until brown. Taste meat, if not tender cover and simmer for 30 to 40 minutes over low heat.

Turn heat up, add vegetables toss until vegetables are tender crisp, about 10 minutes.

Mix cornstarch with water, add to pan, stir and cook until thickened.

Add tomatoes and heat thoroughly.

MEATBALLS

Bonnie Swecker

In medium bowl, mix well:

1 pkg. Italian meatball mix
1/2 c. warm water
1 egg

Let stand 2 minutes. Mix in 1 pound ground beef. (I double my ground beef.)

Pour Ragu' meat sauce in bottom of baking dish. Shape meat mixture into balls, put into dish and pour Ragu' sauce over top of meatballs.

Bake at 350° for 1 hour.

ORIENTAL SHRIMP AND EGGS

1 1/4 lbs. fresh shrimp, or 1 lb. frozen deveined shelled shrimp
1 tsp. dried basil leaves
1/2 tsp. salt
1/2 tsp. pepper
1 (16 oz.) can bean sprouts
1/2 c. butter or margarine
1/2 c. sliced celery
1/2 c. chopped green onions
9 eggs
1/4 c. milk or cream
1/2 tsp. salt

Sprinkle shrimp with 1 teaspoon dry basil leaves, salt, pepper. Rinse and drain bean sprouts under cold water. In large heavy skillet over medium high heat (or electric skillet at 350°), heat butter until foamy.

Add shrimp and celery. Cook, stirring 3 minutes, add drained bean sprouts and onions. Cook 2 minutes longer. Reduce heat to low (300°).

Beat eggs with milk, and a dash of pepper and salt, until blended. Pour over shrimp. Cook, stirring from bottom as eggs set, until all are done. Serve immediately.

Serves 6.

COUNTRY CHICKEN N' BISCUITS

Aunt Oleta

- 8 slices bacon, fried crisp, crumbled
- 2 1/2 c. cooked, cubed chicken
- 1 pkg. frozen mixed vegetables, cooked/drained
- 1 c. chopped tomatoes
- 1 1/2 c. shredded Cheddar cheese
- 1 can cream of chicken soup
- 3/4 c. milk
- 1 1/2 c. Bisquick
- 2/3 c. milk
- 1 can Durkee French fried onion rings

Grease an 8 x 12-inch dish.

Combine first 4 ingredients and 1 cup cheese. Put in dish. Blend soup and 3/4 cup milk, pour over casserole.

Bake, covered, at 400° for 15 minutes.

Meanwhile, combine biscuit mix, milk and 1/2 can French fried onion rings; mix well. Drop by rounded spoonfuls to form 6 biscuits around edge of casserole.

Bake, uncovered, 12-20 minutes or till biscuits are golden brown. Top with remaining cheese and onions and bake 2-3 minutes till onions are tender.

CHICKEN ADOBO

Bonnie's

For 1 chicken:

- 1/4 c. vinegar
- 3 cloves garlic
- 1/8 c. soy sauce
- black pepper (corns, if you have)

Cook over low flame.

LEFT-OVER HAM SUPPER

Bonnie's

2 c. ham strips
2 Tbsp. butter
1 pkg. long grain and wild rice mix with seasonings
No. 2 can Dole pineapple chunks
water

Brown ham strips in butter. Add rice mix with seasonings. Drain syrup from pineapple chunks. Add water to make 2 1/2 cups. Stir into skillet. Cover, cook until liquid is absorbed. Add pineapple chunks.

CRAB QUICHE LORRAINE

Dottie Rockstroh

9-inch pie crust (slightly prebaked)
4 eggs
2 c. light cream (table cream)
2 Tbsp. minced onion
1 tsp. salt
1/8 tsp. red pepper
1 (7 oz.) can crabmeat, drained and cartilage removed
1 c. shredded Mozzarella
parsley flakes

(Keep crust refrigerated.)

Beat eggs till blended. Stir in cream, onion, salt and red pepper. Cover and refrigerate.

About 1 hour before serving, heat oven to 425°. Sprinkle crabmeat and cheese in pie shell. Pour egg mixture over crab/cheese; sprinkle parsley on top.

Bake at 425° for 15 minutes. Reduce oven temperature to 300° and bake 30 minutes longer or till a knife inserted 1-inch from edge comes out clean.

Let quiche stand for 10 minutes before cutting.

HOT CRUNCHY CHICKEN OR TURKEY

Linda Cole

10 3/4 oz. condensed cream of chicken soup
1/4 c. water
2 c. cooked, cubed chicken or turkey
1/4 c. coarsely chopped cashews (optional)
1/2 green pepper, chopped
2 stalks celery, chopped
1 small onion, diced
3 oz. can (2 c.) chow mein noodles

Heat oven to 350°.

PROVOLONE CHICKEN

Linda Cole

6 boneless chicken breasts
hot mustard
12 slices Provolone cheese
Ragu' or favorite spaghetti sauce
Italian seasonings

On each breast place a slice of cheese, spread a layer of hot mustard and sprinkle with Italian seasoning. Roll breast and hold in place with toothpick.

Brown quickly in hot skillet with small amount of oil. Place chicken in 1 1/2-quart baking dish, cover with favorite spaghetti sauce. Top with remaining cheese.

Cover and bake at 350° for 1 hour. Serve over noodles or rice, if desired.

SKILLET CHICKEN AND DUMPLIN'S

Aunt Oleta

Serves 4-6.

2-3 lb. chicken
1 c. Bisquick
2 tsp. salt
1 tsp. paprika
1/8 tsp. pepper
2 Tbsp. shortening
1 Tbsp. butter
2 cans cream of chicken soup
3 c. milk
dumplin' dough
1/2 tsp. parsley flakes
1/4 tsp. poultry seasoning

Mix baking mix, salt, paprika and pepper in plastic bag. Shake chicken. Melt shortening and butter in skillet. Brown chicken. Remove chicken. Stir in soup and milk. Put back chicken. Cover and simmer for about 45 minutes.

But 20 minutes before chicken is done, prepare dumpling dough, adding parsley flakes and poultry seasoning. Drop dough by spoonfuls onto hot chicken.

Cook, uncovered, for 10 minutes, then cook covered 10 minutes longer.

HAMBURGER STROGANOFF

Misty Frye

1 lb. hamburger
1 small chopped onion
1 (4 oz.) can mushrooms, drained
1 can cream of mushroom soup
1/4 c. water or beef broth
1/2 c. sour cream
salt and pepper to taste

Brown hamburger and onion. Drain well. Stir in mushrooms, soup and water. Cover and simmer for 15 to 20 minutes. Stir in sour cream, heat through, but do not let mixture boil. Serve over noodles. Makes 4-5 servings.

KIELBASA CASSEROLE

Aunt Oleta

Serves 6.

1 1/2 qts. chopped, cooked potatoes (8-10 potatoes)
7 slices American cheese
1/4 c. green onion
1/4 c. Wish-Bone blended Italian dressing <u>or</u> Kraft golden blend Italian dressing
2 Tbsp. chopped pimento
1 lb. kielbasa

Mix first 5 ingredients lightly. Spoon into 13 x 9-inch baking dish. Top with kielbasa cut into 6 portions.

Bake at 350° for 30 minutes. Top with cheese slices cut diagonally.

CROCK-POT CHICKEN TERIYAKI

Barbara Weide

1/4 c. brown sugar
1/4 c. soy sauce
3 Tbsp. lemon juice
3 Tbsp. water
1/4 tsp. garlic powder
dash ground ginger
1 cut-up fryer
1/4 c. flour
1/4 c. water

Mix first 6 ingredients until smooth. Pour over chicken, cover and refrigerate several hours or overnight, turning occasionally.

Place chicken and marinade in Crock-Pot, cover. Cook on low 6 to 8 hours or until tender. If thicker gravy is desired, make a paste of 1/4 cup flour and 1/4 cup water, stir into Crock-Pot, cover, cook on high 15 minutes or until thickened.

SHRIMP CREOLE

Joye Moody

1/3 c. salad oil
1 medium onion, chopped
1 small green pepper, chopped
2 stalks celery
2 c. tomatoes
1 1/2 c. cooked shrimp
1/2 tsp. salt
1/2 tsp. garlic salt
1/8 tsp. cayenne pepper
1/2 tsp. chili powder
dash Tabasco sauce
1 tsp. sugar

Heat oil, peel and chop vegetables. Saute until tender, add tomatoes and seasonings. Cook gently, add shrimp and heat thoroughly. Serve over rice.

SLOPPY JOE MIX

Gail Frye

1 lb. hamburger
1/2 c. chopped celery
1/2 c. chopped onion
1/4 c. chopped green pepper
1 clove garlic, minced
2 c. canned tomatoes
1/4 tsp. chili powder
1 tsp. Worcestershire sauce
salt to taste

Brown hamburger. Drain fat. Add celery, onions, green pepper and garlic. Cook for 5 minutes. Add tomatoes and seasonings. Cover and simmer for 30 minutes.

CREPES

Kris Miller

1 1/2 c. flour
1 Tbsp. sugar
1/2 tsp. salt
2 c. milk
2 eggs
1/2 tsp. vanilla
2 Tbsp. margarine (for pan)

Combine ingredients and mix with wire whisk. Melt margarine in pan under medium heat. Dip enough batter to cover bottom of pan. It will make a thin "pancake".

After first side is cooked, gently flip over and cook other side 1 to 2 minutes. Remove from pan. Set aside to cool.

Crepes may be filled as other crepes are cooking. Place jelly, jam or preserves on 1/2 of crepe in a thin layer. Roll up and dust lightly with powdered sugar if desired.

*Sliced fruit, seafood salad, broccoli and cheese or filling of your choice can be used instead of jelly, jam or preserves.

STUFFED GREEN PEPPERS

Misty Frye

8-10 green peppers
1 c. uncooked rice
1 Tbsp. oil
1 lb. hamburger
1/4 c. chopped onion
1/4 c. chopped bell pepper
1 1/2 tsp. salt
1/2 tsp. pepper

Core green peppers and par boil for 2-3 minutes. Drain. Cook rice. Brown hamburger with oil, onion and chopped bell pepper. Drain fat.

Add rice, salt and pepper; mix well. Stuff peppers with mixture and bake at 350° for 30 minutes.

SCHEERER SLOPP — Paula Scheerer

1 large can Manwich sloppy joe mix
2 lbs. ground beef, cooked and drained
1 lb. frozen corn
1 box macaroni and cheese mix, prepared
3 Tbsp. hot barbecue sauce
1 large onion, chopped
1 large can mushrooms

Prepare ground beef and Manwich. Stir in chopped onions and mushrooms. Simmer.

Prepare frozen corn.

Prepare macaroni and cheese.

After all ingredients are prepared, mix all together in a large bowl, stir in barbecue sauce and serve over toast or crunchy noodles.

HAM LOAF — Mary Rowe

1 lb. cured ham, ground
1 lb. fresh pork, ground
2 eggs
2/3 c. cracker crumbs
1/3 c. Minute Tapioca
1 1/4 c. milk

Dressing:

1/4 c. vinegar
1/2 c. water
1/2 c. brown sugar
1 Tbsp. prepared mustard

Mix first 6 ingredients and form into a loaf. Then mix ingredients for dressing and boil together for a few minutes. Pour dressing over loaf and bake, covered, at 350°-400° about 2 hours, basting occasionally.

Dressing should become thick and syrupy. (If put in single loaf pan, it will not need basting.) This needs to be covered when baking or brown sugar will turn black and hard.

DOWN HOME STUFFIN CASSEROLE — Portia Mae Morris

2 pkgs. Stove Top stuffing mix
butter
1 can chicken mushroom cream soup
3/4 c. milk
8 boneless chicken breasts
flour
2 eggs, slightly beaten
(fried chicken seasoning)

Prepare stuffing mix according to directions. Dip chicken in eggs and dredge in seasoned flour.

ONION BAKED MEATLOAF

Sherry Heward

1 1/2 lbs. ground beef
1 tsp. salt
1/3 tsp. black pepper
1 egg, slightly beaten
1 c. soft bread crumbs
1 c. milk
1 c. chopped onion
1 c. tomato juice
1 Tbsp. cornstarch
1 onion, peeled, sliced
oil
paprika

1. In a large bowl, mix beef well. Add salt, pepper and egg.
2. Mix bread crumbs and milk, let stand a few minutes.
3. Add bread crumbs to meat and mix in chopped onions and tomato juice.
4. Add cornstarch. Blend well.
5. Turn mixture into well-greased 9 by 5 by 3-inch loaf pan.
6. Bake at 350° for about 1 hour.
7. Add sliced onion when 15 minutes of baking time remains. Brush onions with oil and sprinkle with paprika. Bake meatloaf until center is done.

FRENCH HAMBURGERS

Sherry Heward

1 lb. lean ground beef
1 1/2 tsp. ground sage
1 1/4 tsp. each: salt and pepper
2 green onions, whites and greens, finely chopped
1 egg, whipped
2 Tbsp. oil

1. Break up the meat with a fork, mixing in the sage, salt and pepper, green onions.
2. Thoroughly whip egg and mix with meat mixture.
3. Let stand 30 minutes to blend flavors.
4. Shape into 4 to 8 patties.
5. Heat the oil until hot in heavy skillet. Add patties, turning down the heat to medium.
6. Cook for 3 to 4 minutes, depending on size of patties.
7. Turn up the heat. Flip the patties. Cook another 3 to 4 minutes, heat turned down after browning.

YORKSHIRE CHICKEN

Sherry Heward

1 frying chicken (3 to 3 1/2 lb.), cut up
1 1/3 c. all-purpose flour, divided
2 tsp. salt, divided
1 tsp. poultry seasoning
1/4 tsp. pepper
1/2 c. butter or margarine, divided
1 tsp. baking powder
3 eggs
1 1/2 c. milk

1. Mix 1/3 cup flour, 1 teaspoon salt, the poultry seasoning and pepper.
2. Coat chicken pieces with the mixture.
3. Brown all sides in 1/4 cup butter in large skillet.
4. Arrange chicken in a 13 by 9-inch baking pan.
5. Bake at 350° for 30 minutes.
6. Remove chicken. If desired, make gravy in pan, using drippings. Pour into saucepan.
7. Put chicken back in pan.
8. In mixer, beat together remaining flour, salt, baking powder, eggs and milk. Add remaining butter, melted. Beat until smooth.
9. Pour over chicken. Bake at 350° for another 45 minutes.

SKILLET CHICKEN WITH BISCUIT DUMPLING

Sherry Heward

1 frying chicken (3 to 3 1/2 lb.), cut up
1/2 tsp. salt
1 tsp. paprika
1/4 c. butter or margarine
1 (10 3/4 oz.) can condensed chicken broth
1 Tbsp. instant minced onion
1/2 tsp. poultry seasoning
1/8 tsp. black pepper
3 c. frozen peas and carrots, thawed
1 (8 oz.) pkg. refrigerated buttermilk biscuits

1. Sprinkle chicken pieces on both sides with salt and paprika.
2. Melt butter in a large skillet. Add chicken pieces and saute until well browned on both sides.
3. Remove chicken and pour off drippings. Return chicken to skillet. Add enough water to broth to make 1 1/2 cups. Pour over chicken.
4. Add minced onion, poultry seasonings and black pepper to pan. Bring to boil. Cover and simmer 25 minutes.
5. Add vegetables and bring to boiling again. Top with biscuits. Simmer uncovered 10 minutes. Cover and simmer 10 minutes longer.

HONEY CHICKEN

Portia Mae Morris

1/2 c. honey
1/2 c. prepared mustard
1/4 c. butter or margarine, melted
1 tsp. curry powder
3 lbs. chicken breasts, boneless, skinless

Combine first 4 ingredients - set aside. Dip each piece of chicken in sauce and place in large greased roasting pan. Pour remaining sauce over chicken.

Bake at 350° for 1 hour. Serve with fried rice.

TUNA PATTIES

Julie Burnham

1 (6 oz.) pkg. chicken-flavor stuffing
1/2 c. hot water
1 can cream of chicken soup (undiluted and divided)
2 eggs, beaten
1 (9 1/4 oz.) can tuna, drained and flaked
3 Tbsp. melted butter
1/4 c. milk

Remove vegetable seasoning packet and stuffing crumbs from package. Combine vegetable seasoning and water. Stir well. Add crumbs, half of soup, eggs and tuna. Blend well. Form into 6 patties and brown in butter.

Combine remaining soup and milk. Heat thoroughly. Serve as sauce.

Note: Sometimes when I boil the vegetable seasoning packet with the water, I like to add one stalk of chopped celery.

HAMBURGER AND BEANS

Mary Parsons

1 lb. ground beef
1 onion, diced
1/3 c. honey
2 Tbsp. cinnamon
2 (15 oz.) cans vegetarian beans or pork and beans

Over low heat, brown ground beef and saute onions together. Drain fat. Pour honey over beef and onion mixture, sprinkle with cinnamon. Stir over low heat, add beans, heat to desired temperature.

Serves 4.

SAUSAGE QUICHE

Linda Murphy

1 (9-inch) unbaked pie crust
1/2-3/4 lb. bulk pork sausage
1/2 c. chopped onion
1 1/2 c. (6 oz.) shredded sharp cheese
2 Tbsp. flour
2 tsp. parsley flakes
2 eggs, beaten
1 small can evaporated milk

Preheat oven to 375°. Fully cook sausage. Drain well.

Combine sausage, onion, cheese, flour and parsley flakes. Mix well. Spread in unbaked pie crust.

Beat together eggs and evaporated milk. Slowly pour over sausage mixture.

Bake on preheated cookie sheet 35-40 minutes or until filling is set.

COLLEGE PIE

English dinner, 15 minutes to make.

2 or 3 lbs. ground beef, lean
1 can stewed tomatoes
4 Tbsp. Worcestershire sauce
1 large onion, chopped
2 tsp. hot pepper juice
2 1/2 Tbsp. Bisto gravy mix*

*Bisto gravy has no fats in it, found at Safeway Store.

Brown beef in skillet. Drain off all fat and water in drainer. Brown onions with meat. Pour in can of stewed tomatoes, also hot pepper juice. Mix well. Pour in Worcestershire sauce, mix. In large cup mix gravy mix with 1 cup of water. Have water boiling to add enough to make gravy as thick as you want it. Let simmer for 5 minutes.

This can be served over rice; or with mashed potatoes on top in a oven-safe dish and potatoes browned in oven for 10 minutes at 400°.

Serves 6-8 people. Very budget stretching dinner.

WESTERN STYLE STRINGBEANS

Lois Middleton

1 1/2 lbs. ground chuck or sirloin
2 cans string beans, drained
2 cans sliced potatoes
2 or 3 cans tomato sauce
1 onion, sliced

Brown ground meat in large frying pan or Dutch oven pan. Add string beans (drained). Add 2 cans tomato sauce, sliced onion, 2 cans potatoes. Cook about 30 minutes. If more sauce is needed, add 1 can. Simmer low for about 30 more minutes. Makes a great 1 dish meal.

HOTCH POTCH

Sherry Heward

1 lb. beef
1 (10 1/2 oz.) can beef broth plus water to make 2 c.
4 medium carrots, peeled
3 medium potatoes, peeled and quartered
3 medium onions, halved
1 small head cauliflower
2 Tbsp. butter or margarine
salt and pepper
1 Tbsp. cornstarch
2 Tbsp. cold water

1. Trim fat from meat. Cut meat into 1 1/2 inch cubes. Put meat in large heavy pan. Add beef broth. Bring to a boil. Cover and simmer for 45 minutes or until almost tender.
2. Add carrots, potatoes and onions. Bring to boil. Cover and cook for 20 minutes or until all are tender. Add cauliflower. Cover and cook 10 minutes longer.
3. Remove vegetables. Add butter, salt and black pepper to taste. Thicken juices with cornstarch blended with 2 tablespoons cold water.
4. Serve meat and gravy with vegetables.

BAKED CHICKEN AND POTATOES

Sherlie Hale

1 pkg. chicken
1 can cream of chicken soup
1 can Heinz chicken gravy
5 medium potatoes
3 large carrots
2 stalks celery

(Place chicken in 9 x 12 pan.) Bake chicken until crispy. Bake at 400° for 45 minutes.

In medium bowl, mix gravy and soup together. Chop celery, wedge carrots and quarter potatoes. Boil potatoes, celery and carrots on stove top 10-15 minutes. Add to chicken when chicken has been baked to your satisfaction. Pour on gravy and bake for approximately 5-8 minutes.

Serves 4.

CRAB-SHRIMP BAKE

Linda Cole
Sherlie Hale

1 c. cooked shrimp (4 1/2-5 oz. can)
1 c. diced celery
1/4 c. chopped green peppers
2 Tbsp. fine chopped onion
7 1/2 oz. crab meat
1/2 tsp. salt
dash pepper
1 tsp. Worcestershire sauce
3/4 c. mayonnaise
1 Tbsp. butter
1 c. bread crumbs (soft)

Combine clean cooked shrimp, dice celery, chopped peppers, chopped onion, crab meat (drained, flaked and cartilage removed), salt, pepper, Worcestershire sauce and mayonnaise. Turn into 1-quart casserole dish.

Combine bread crumbs with melted butter. Sprinkle on top of casserole. Bake at 350° for 30-35 minutes.

(Serves 4.)

STUFFED SHRIMP

Linda Cole
Sherlie Hale

1 lb. large raw shrimp in shells (16 shrimp)
3/4 c. rich round cracker crumbs
3 Tbsp. butter, melted
1 (7 1/2 oz.) can crabmeat
2 Tbsp. snipped parsley
1/2 tsp. garlic powder
1/3 c. white grape juice
1/2 tsp. salt and dash pepper

Shell and devein shrimp. Split each along vein side about halfway through. Combine crumbs and butter. Stir in crabmeat, parsley, garlic powder, salt and pepper. Stuff each shrimp with crab mixture.

Arrange on baking dish, 12 x 7 1/2 x 2-inch. Bake at 350° for 18-20 minutes. Baste occasionally with grape juice.

(Serves 4.)

SWEET AND SOUR SHRIMP

Misty Frye

1 1/2 lbs. cooked shrimp
1/2 c. sliced carrots
1/2 c. sliced water chestnuts
1/2 c. chopped green peppers, chunks
1/2 c. sugar
1/3 c. ketchup
1 Tbsp. soy sauce
1/4 tsp. salt
1 c. water, divided
3 1/2 Tbsp. cornstarch
1/2 c. vinegar
1 (15 1/4 oz.) can unsweetened pineapple chunks, drained

Cook carrots and chestnuts in boiling water for 2 minutes. Add green pepper and boil an additional 1-2 minutes. Drain and place in cold water.

In a saucepan, combine sugar, ketchup, soy sauce, salt

and 2/3 cup of water. Bring to boil. Mix 1/3 cup water with cornstarch to make a paste. Gradually add paste and vinegar to saucepan. Cook, stirring constantly until smooth and thick. Remove from heat. Drain vegetables. Add vegetables, pineapple chunks and shrimp. Place on low heat until well heated (stir frequently). Serve over rice. Serves 6 people.

AUNT LOUISE'S CHICKEN PIE **Kris Leonard**

4 c. diced chicken
3/4 c. butter
3/4 c. flour
1 tsp. salt
1/8 tsp. pepper
2 c. chicken stock
2 c. light cream
1 Tbsp. lemon juice

Melt butter, add flour, cream and stock slowly, stirring constantly, cook 15 minutes until thickened and there is not starchy taste.

Remove from heat, add lemon juice and chicken, salt, pepper. Pour into 2-quart oblong pan.

Batter Topping:

1 1/4 c. flour
1/2 tsp. salt
2 tsp. pepper
4 eggs, separated
1 c. milk
2 Tbsp. melted butter

Mix together, beating egg whites separately; fold in, pour over chicken.

Bake at 425° for 12-15 minutes.

STUFFED CHICKEN BREASTS **Ken Carter**

8 boneless, skinless chicken breasts
1 pkg. Stove Top stuffing mix, prepared as directed
1/2 apple, peeled and finely chopped
1/4 c. slivered almonds
1/3 c. raisins
pkg. white sauce mix, prepared as directed

Flatten chicken breasts. Mix together all other ingredients. Put a big spoonful of stuffing on each breast. Roll 'em up, securing with toothpicks.

Bake at 325° for 40 minutes or till done. Pour white sauce over chicken breasts.

SPEEDY SAUERBRATEN

Kris Leonard

3 lb. rolled rump or chuck roast
1/3 c. grape jelly
2 large onions, sliced
6 whole black peppers
2 crushed bay leaves
2 tsp. salt
1/3 c. vinegar
1/2 tsp. allspice
1/4 tsp. pepper
1/4 c. water
1 tsp. Kitchen Bouquet

Trim excess fat from meat, brown slowly, spread with grape jelly, top with onions and seasonings.

Combine vinegar, water and Kitchen Bouquet and pour over meat.

Cook slowly over medium-low heat, as pot roast.

SAUERBRATEN MEATBALLS

Kris Leonard

1 lb. ground beef
1/2 c. bread crumbs
1 small onion, chopped
1 egg
salt, pepper
2 Tbsp. flour
1/2 tsp. ginger
2 beef bouillon cubes
1 1/2 c. water
1 small can mushrooms
1/4 c. brown sugar
2 Tbsp. lemon juice

Mix and shape beef, bread crumbs, onion, egg, salt and pepper into meatballs. Brown in skillet.

Add everything else, mixing well. Simmer over low heat, 15-20 minutes, adding more water if necessary.

Serve over rice.

CRAB IMPERIAL

Mrs. Sam Gladwin

1 lb. crab meat
2 slices bread crumbs
4 Tbsp. mayonnaise
1 tsp. prepared mustard
dash Worcestershire sauce
1/2 tsp. chopped parsley
1 Tbsp. green pepper, chopped
1 tsp. Old Bay seasoning

Sauce:

1 1/2 Tbsp. butter or margarine
1 Tbsp. cornstarch
1 c. milk
salt and pepper (dash)

Saute green peppers. Prepare sauce and combine all ingredients adding crab meat last. Put into individual serving dishes (oven-proof) or bake in casserole dish.

Bake at 350° for 15 to 20 minutes or till light brown on top.

COQ AU VIN (CHICKEN IN WINE)

Kris Leonard

1 frying chicken, cut in pieces
flour
1/2 lb. fresh mushrooms, cleaned
1 1/2-2 c. red or rose wine
bouquet garni - little parsley, thyme, bay leaf - tied together in cheesecloth

Shake chicken in flour, brown in butter in a large pot, add mushrooms, bouquet garni, wine.

Cook over medium-low heat about 1 hour.

BEEF MEXICANA

Betty Adelung

1 lb. cooked ground beef
1 can corn
1 large onion, diced
1 green pepper, diced
sugar (use judgement)
salt and pepper to taste
1/2 tsp. garlic salt
1/2 tsp. oregano
Minute Rice

Combine all ingredients except rice. Simmer about 1 hour. Serve over prepared rice.

EASY CHICKEN DINNER

Betty Adelung

chicken parts (your preference)
McCormick's Season-All
McCormick's herb seasoning
McCormick's chicken seasoning
2 pats butter or margarine

1. Place chicken parts (with or without skin) in shallow sheet pan.
2. Add enough water to cover bottom of pan (about 1/4-inch deep).
3. Sprinkle chicken with all three spices. Add butter pats to water to keep from sticking.
4. Broil 1/2 hour, turn chicken and repeat steps 3 and 4.

BOEUF BOURGUIGNON

Joye Moody

1 lb. round roast, cubed
1/2 can consomme
1/2 c. red wine
1 chopped onion
1 whole bay leaf
thyme
1 large clove
2-3 Tbsp. butter

Brown butter, saute onions, brown meat, add everything else, cook slowly on top of stove 2 1/2 hours, thicken sauce, remove herbs. Serve over rice or noodles.

FRIED CHICKEN

Jenny Moody

Seasoning:

2-3 c. flour
large handful salt
1 tsp. pepper
2 tsp. chicken bouillon
1 tsp. oregano
1 tsp. thyme
1 tsp. poultry seasoning
1/4 tsp. garlic
2 tsp. parsley
2 tsp. minced onion

Shake seasonings together in plastic bag or large piece of Tupperware.

Shake chicken pieces in seasoning. Fry in 1/4-1/2 inch oil, turning to brown.

Store leftover seasoning in refrigerator until next use.

GRILLED SHRIMP OR SCALLOPS

Bonnie Carter

1/3 c. margarine
1/2 tsp. curry powder
1/2 tsp. garlic powder
1/2 tsp. pepper
1/4 c. dried parsley
2 lbs. raw shrimp, peeled and deveined or scallops

Cream butter with remaining ingredients except seafood. Divide seafood equally on 6 pieces of heavy-duty aluminum foil. Top each with butter mixture. Bring foil up around seafood; seal tightly.

Place foil packets directly on hot coals. Cook 10-15 minutes. Serve in foil packages.

MEXICALI CHILIBURGER SKILLET

Misty Frye

1 lb. hamburger
1 c. chopped onion
1 large can chopped whole tomatoes
1 can tomato sauce
1 tsp. oregano
1 tsp. salt
chili powder to taste
pepper to taste
1 can corn
1 c. macaroni, uncooked
1/2 c. water
1/2 c. shredded Cheddar cheese

Brown hamburger and drain. Stir in onion, tomatoes, tomato sauce and spices. Heat to boiling. Add undrained corn, uncooked macaroni and water. Bring to a boil. Cover and simmer 15-20 minutes or until macaroni is tender. Sprinkle on cheese, cover again until cheese is melted.

QUICK 'N' EASY SALMON PATTIES

Madeline Nelson
(Kris Miller's Mom)

1 (15 to 16 oz.) can pink salmon
1 egg
1/3 c. minced onion
1/2 c. flour
1 1/2 tsp. baking powder
1 1/2 c. Crisco

Drain salmon; set aside 2 tablespoons of the juice. In a medium mixing bowl, mix salmon, egg and onion until sticky. Stir in flour. Add baking powder to salmon juice; stir into salmon mixture. Form into small patties and fry until golden brown (about 5 minutes) in hot Crisco.

Serves 4 to 6.

SWEET AND SOUR MEATBALLS

Madeline Nelson
(Kris Miller's Mom)

1 lb. lean ground beef
2 eggs, slightly beaten
1 medium onion, finely chopped
1/2 c. seasoned, dry bread crumbs
1/2 tsp. salt
1/2 tsp. black pepper
1 tsp. soy sauce
dash ground oregano
1/4 c. shortening
1 (6 oz.) can pineapple chunks, undrained
3/4 c. sugar
1/3 c. cider vinegar
2 Tbsp. cornstarch
2 Tbsp. dark soy sauce

Combine first 9 ingredients; mix well and shape into 1-inch balls. Brown in hot shortening in a heavy skillet over medium heat. Drain well.

Drain pineapple, reserving juice; add water to make 1/3 cup liquid. Combine 1/3 cup liquid, sugar, vinegar, cornstarch and dark soy sauce in a saucepan. Cook over medium heat until thickened and bubbly. Add pineapple and meatballs, stir to coat. Stir in a chafing dish.

Makes 3 1/2 dozen.

SUPER SIMPLE MEAT LOAF

Nancy Dove

1 1/2 lbs. ground beef
1 c. packed herb-seasoned stuffing
1 c. tomato juice
1/2 c. chopped onion
1 egg

In bowl, combine all ingredients; mix well. Shape into loaf; place in shallow baking pan. Bake at 350°F. for 1 1/4 hours. Serves 6.

If desired, cover loaf with 2 tablespoons ketchup before baking.

HUNGARIAN GOULASH

Madeline Nelson
(Kris Miller's Mom)

1/2 c. flour
1/2 tsp. each: salt and pepper
pinch Hungarian paparika
2 1/2-3 lbs. round steak, cut into 1-inch cubes
3 Tbsp. vegetable oil
2 Tbsp. melted margarine
6 chopped onions
2 c. beef broth, divided
3 Tbsp. tomato paste
1 Tbsp. Hungarian paprika
grated rind of 1 lemon
1/2 tsp. marjoram
1/4 tsp. caraway seeds
1 clove garlic, crushed
hot buttered noodles

Combine first 4 ingredients; stir well. Dredge meat in flour mixture and saute in oil and margarine until well browned. Drain well. Reserve drippings.

Saute onion in drippings until tender; drain well. Combine onion, 1/3 cup broth, tomato paste, 1 tablespoon paprika, lemon rind, marjoram, seeds and garlic in a large Dutch oven; simmer 3 minutes. Stir in meat and remaining broth, cover and simmer 1 1/2 hours or until meat is tender. Serve on noodles.

Makes 10 servings.

ONION-MUSHROOM MEATLOAF

Kris Miller

2 lbs. ground beef
1 1/2 c. soft bread crumbs
2 eggs
1 envelope Lipton onion-mushroom soup mix
3/4 c. water
1/3 c. ketchup
dash Worcestershire sauce

Preheat oven to 350°.

In large bowl, combine all ingredients. In large baking pan shape into loaf. Cover with aluminum foil and bake for 1 hour or until done. Makes 8 to 10 servings.

For variation, add 1 small can of drained mushroom pieces to meatloaf mixture.

SWEET AND SOUR TURKEY

Kris Miller

1 pkg. turkey drumsticks or other turkey meat of your choice (wing or breast)
4 Tbsp. applesauce
4 Tbsp. cider vinegar
4 Tbsp. honey
3 Tbsp. soy sauce
garlic powder
1 1/2 c. crushed pineapple

Place turkey legs in pan and cook in broiler until skin is crisp. Sprinkle with garlic powder. Combine remaining ingredients and pour over turkey. Cover pan and bake at 350°F. for 1 1/2 hours, basting occasionally.

ORANGE GLAZED HAM

Kris Miller

3 lb. boneless, precooked ham
1/2 c. brown sugar
1 tsp. dry mustard
1 tsp. grated orange peel (spice) and 2 Tbsp. orange juice
whole cloves (enough to stud top of ham)

Mix all ingredients in mixing bowl except cloves and ham. Stir together. Score top of ham and stud with whole cloves. Place in baking pan (covered pan preferred or "tent" aluminum foil and cover pan).

Preheat oven to 350°. Bake ham for 1 hour (last hour baste with glaze).

BEEF PEPPER STEAK

Kris Miller

1/4 c. vegetable oil
1 lb. round steak, cut into thin strips (partially frozen meat is easier to slice)
1 thinly sliced medium onion
1 Tbsp. cornstarch
1/2 c. cold water
1 tsp. sugar
2 Tbsp. soy sauce
1 tsp. garlic salt
1/4 tsp. black pepper

Preheat oil in electric skillet, uncovered, at 325°. Add meat and brown. Remove to serving dish. Add onion and pepper slices to skillet and cook until just tender. Dissolve cornstarch in water and soy sauce. Add sugar, garlic salt and pepper. Pour into skillet with vegetables, stirring until sauce is thickened and clear. Add meat and cook several minutes longer or until heated through. Serve over hot rice.

Makes approximately 4 servings.

CHICKEN-BROCCOLI-CAULIFLOWER CASSEROLE

Kris Miller

2 boxes frozen broccoli spears
2 boxes frozen cauliflower
2 or more c. cooked chicken, cut up
2 cans cream of chicken soup
1 can milk
1 box Stove Top stuffing
Swiss cheese
salt and pepper

Cook and drain vegetables. Place chicken, cauliflower, broccoli in pan. Salt and pepper as desired. Pour milk and soup over chicken. Put thin layer of Swiss cheese over top. Prepare box of Stove Top stuffing. Spoon over top.

Bake at 350°, uncovered, for 30-35 minutes.

TURKEY BAR-B-Q

Kris Miller

This recipe is great for leftover turkey - a great alternative to turkey salad.

turkey meat (dark and/or light from leftover turkey) 2 to 5 c., cut into strips or pieces
2 c. ketchup
2 c. water
2 c. chopped onion
2 Tbsp. vinegar
2 Tbsp. Worcestershire sauce
2 tsp. mustard
2 Tbsp. lemon
2 tsp. oregano
2 tsp. basil
1/4 tsp. black pepper
dash salt
1/3 (or more to taste) brown sugar or 1/3 c. honey

Combine all ingredients, adding turkey last, simmer over medium heat until barbecue boils, reduce heat; simmer 10 minutes. Serve over rice or with rolls.

Dark meat is better used in this recipe.

SWEET AND SOUR MEATBALLS

Sharon Hale

3 lbs. hamburger
1 1/2 c. bread crumbs
3 eggs
1 1/4 c. milk
4 Tbsp. grated onion
3 tsp. salt
1 tsp. pepper
1 tsp. oregano leaves
1 tsp. garlic powder

Sauce:

2 large ketchup
1 c. grape jelly
1/4 tsp. garlic powder

Preheat oven to 350°.

Mix hamburger, bread crumbs, eggs and milk with a spoon or use your hands. Then add grated onion, salt, pepper, oregano leaves and garlic powder. Mix it all together, then roll with hands in meatballs, they can be any size you desire. Place on cookie sheets in oven after 2 minutes turn meatballs over and allow to cook 3 minutes or until browned.

Sauce: In a slow cooker or on stove top pour in the 2 large bottles of ketchup, jelly and garlic powder; stir occasionally; adjust temperature as needed for the jelly to melt and mix well. After jelly has all melted add meatballs and have it cook on lower at least 1 hour so flavor will get into your meatballs.

SHRIMP CREOLE

Kris Miller

1 onion
2 Tbsp. margarine
1 c. sliced green pepper
1/2 c. celery
1 tsp. parsley
1 tsp. salt
1/8 tsp. cayenne pepper
16 oz. can tomato paste
2 c. water
2 c. cooked shrimp, deveined and shelled

Cook onions in margarine. Stir in remaining ingredients except shrimp. Cook over low heat. Simmer 15 minutes. Add shrimp, simmer for an additional 10-15 minutes on low heat. Serve over rice if desired.

CHILI AND BEANS

Shirley Necessary

1 lb. ground chuck or round
1 onion
2 packs Chili-O mix (McCormick's)
2 cans red kidney beans
2 cans whole tomatoes (16 oz.)
salt and pepper (to taste)
4 c. water

Fry beef with onions until done (drain off any fat). In large pot, cook tomatoes and water and Chili-O mix (mash tomatoes). Cook for about 30 minutes.

Add beans and beef; cook for about 10 more minutes. Salt and pepper to taste.

SWEDISH MEATBALLS

Nancy Dove

1 lb. ground beef
1/4 c. fine dry bread crumbs
1/4 c. minced onion
1 egg, slightly beaten
2 Tbsp. chopped parsley
1 (10 1/2 oz.) can condensed cream of celery soup
1/2 soup can water
1 to 2 Tbsp. minced dill pickle

Mix beef, bread crumbs, onion, egg and parsley; shape into 24 meatballs. In skillet, brown meatballs, pour off drippings. Stir in soup, water and pickle. Cover, cook over low heat 20 minutes, stir often. Serve over rice. 4 servings.

Write your extra recipes here:

MAIN DISHES
EGG • CASSEROLE
CHEESE • PASTA

EGG, CHEESE, PASTA AND CASSEROLE

* To prevent eggs from curdling when they are to be added to hot liquid, add a bit of the hot liquid to the eggs first and letting the temperature equalize. Then they can be added to the remaining liquid with no worries.

* Adding vegetable oil to pasta cooking water before you add the pasta will cut down on sticking.

* When preparing your favorite casserole, double the batch and freeze one for a busy day.

* Egg yolks can be kept for several days in the refrigerator if they are covered with vegetable oil.

* If a casserole dish is lined with several layers of foil and then filled and frozen, the casserole can be lifted out when solid and wrapped for freezing without losing the use of the casserole dish. It will fit right back into the dish when it's time to bake it. This also makes for easier stacking of casseroles in the freezer.

* A dull warm knife works best for slicing cheese.

* Use a fry basket in the pot when cooking pasta. The pasta can be lifted out all at once and rinsed in the same basket.

* Stir eggs while they are boiling to keep the yolks centered. This makes deviled eggs prettier.

* Storing cheese in a tightly covered container with a few sugar cubes will retard mold.

* Hardened cheese can be softened by soaking in buttermilk.

* Bring salted water to a boil, stir in pasta, cover and turn off the heat. Check the pot in ten minutes.

* If grater is brushed with oil before you grate cheese clean up will be a snap!

* Adding vinegar to the water used to cook hard boiled eggs will keep them from 'running' if a shell is cracked.

* Rub shortening around the top of the pot to prevent boil overs.

* Mark hard boiled eggs before they are stored so you won't have to guess the raw eggs from the cooked ones. This can be done with a crayon or by adding food coloring to the cooking water.

* Run cooked spaghetti under HOT water to prevent stickiness.

CHEESY POTATO EGG CASSEROLE

Portia Morris

6 large red potatoes (about 2 1/2 lbs.)
1 (10 3/4 oz.) can cream of chicken soup, undiluted
1 (8 oz.) carton sour cream
1/4 tsp. curry powder
1/4 tsp. pepper
4 hard-cooked eggs, chopped
2 Tbsp. fine dry bread crumbs
1 c. shredded Cheddar cheese

Cook potatoes in boiling water 25-30 minutes until tender; drain and cool to touch. Peel and cut into 1/4-inch slices; set aside.

Combine soup, sour cream, curry powder and pepper; mix well. Layer half each of potato slices, eggs and soup mixture in greased 12 x 8 x 2-inch baking dish; repeat layers. Cover and bake at 350° for 30 minutes. Sprinkle with bread crumbs and cheese. Bake, uncovered 5 minutes or until cheese melts.

Serves 8.

EGG CASSEROLE

Portia Morris

4 eggs
3/4 tsp. dry mustard
2 1/2 c. milk
2 lbs. Jimmy Dean hot sausage
3 or 4 c. plain croutons
2 1/2 c. sharp Cheddar cheese, grated
1 can cream of mushroom soup
1/2 can milk

In 9 x 13-inch baking pan spread croutons. Brown sausage and drain. Alternate layers of sausage and cheese on top of croutons.

Beat eggs, mustard and milk, pour on casserole and refrigerate overnight (8 hours).

Before baking, mix soup and 1/2 can milk, pour on casserole. Bake 1 1/2 hours at 300°.

YANCEY'S YEGGS

Carol Riley

Place peach halves with the well up in a baking dish. Place 4 sausage links (precooked) around each peach half. Mix up some cornbread mix according to package directions. Put a glob of batter atop of each peach. Bake until cornbread is done. Serve with scrambled eggs.

(Each peach half etal, is one serving.)

CORN PATCH CASSEROLE

Bonnie Swecker

2 1/2 c. egg noodles
1 can whole kernel corn, drained
1 can cream of vegetable soup
3/4 c. milk
1 can Spam, cut into cubes
sharp cheese, grated or shaved
paprika
1 tsp. salt

Cook noodles in 2 quarts boiling water for 10 minutes. Drain and pour into deep dish, 9-inch casserole.

Mix in corn, soup, milk, salt and Spam. Top with cheese and paprika.

Bake at 350° for 30 minutes.

TUNA CASSEROLE

Bonnie Swecker

1/2 (16 oz.) pkg. noodles
2 Tbsp. oil
1 c. onion, chopped
1/2 c. green pepper, chopped
1 (15 oz.) can tomato sauce
1 c. water
2 tsp. salt
1/2 tsp. garlic powder
1/4 tsp. pepper
2 (7 oz.) cans tuna, drained and flaked
1/2 c. shredded Cheddar cheese, about 2 oz.

Cook noodles according to package directions.

In medium skillet, heat oil and cook onions, green pepper until tender. Stir in tomato sauce, water, salt, garlic powder, pepper and simmer 10 minutes.

In 2-quart casserole, combine noodles, sauce and tuna. Bake 30 minutes in 375° oven or until heated through.

Top with cheese, let stand covered until cheese melts. Makes about 6 servings.

EASY HEART-HEALTHY MANICOTTI

(A do-ahead dish.)

1 1/2 lbs. ground turkey
1 egg (substitute)
1/2 lb. low moisture, part-skim Mozzarella cheese, grated
3 slices moist bread
1/2 c. skim milk
1 tsp. salt
1/2 tsp. pepper
1 Tbsp. parsley
1 tsp. oregano
1 box manicotti shells
giant size jar Ragu' extra-thick and hearty spaghetti sauce (or your favorite brand)

Mix all ingredients <u>except</u> last 2 in a large bowl.

Spray 9 x 13-inch baking pan with an oil spray (Pam).

Spread cup spaghetti sauce in bottom of pan. You should have about a 1/4-inch layer of sauce in the bottom of the pan. Then stuff dry manicotti shells with meat mixture and arrange in pan. Pour enough sauce over stuffed shells to cover them well. Cover pan and let sit in refrigerator overnight.

The next day, bake covered casserole in 350° oven for about 40 minutes.

TOMATO - CARROT SPAGHETTI SAUCE **Julie Burnham**

1 garlic clove, minced
1 green pepper, minced
1/3 c. chopped celery
1 large onion, chopped
3 parsley sprigs
2 medium carrots, diced
2 Tbsp. olive oil

* * * * * * * *

2 1/2 c. chopped fresh or canned (1 (19 oz.) can) tomatoes
2 bay leaves
6 peppercorns
1/4 tsp. thyme
2 tsp. salt
dash cayenne
6 whole cloves
1 tsp. sugar
1 (6 oz.) can tomato paste
1/2 lb. mushrooms, sliced
1 Tbsp. butter or margarine

Put first 7 ingredients in kettle. Cover and cook gently for 15 minutes; do not brown. Stir frequently. Add remaining ingredients except tomato paste, mushrooms and butter. Simmer, covered, for about 45 minutes.

Force through a coarse sieve. Add tomato paste. Saute mushrooms in butter for about 5 minutes.

Serves 4. Can be doubled.

SPINACH CHEESE SOUFFLE

6 eggs
1 lb. cottage cheese (small curd)
2 (10 oz.) pkgs. frozen chopped spinach (thawed and drained), NOT cooked
3/4 lb. white American cheese, grated
3/4 lb. Swiss cheese, grated

Stir all ingredients together. Spread out evenly in 9 x 13 baking dish. Bake at 375° for 45 to 55 minutes. Souffle is done when top is golden brown. Remove from oven, let cool 10 minutes or so before cutting and serving.

EGGPLANT ITALIANO CASSEROLE

1 (1 lb.) can tomatoes
1 (8 oz.) can tomato sauce
1/4 c. celery, chopped
1 small onion, chopped
1/4 tsp. salt
1/4 tsp. leaf oregano, crumbled
1/4 tsp. leaf basil, crumbled
1/8 tsp. leaf sage, crumbled
dash pepper
1 eggplant (about 1/4 lb.), unpared and sliced
1 c. skim milk Ricotta cheese or low-fat cottage cheese
2 Tbsp. grated Parmesan cheese
1 block skim milk Mozzarella, shredded

Combine tomatoes, tomato sauce, celery, onion, salt, oregano, basil, sage, and pepper in a medium-sized saucepan; bring to boil. Lower heat; simmer, uncovered, stirring occasionally for about 30 minutes.

While sauce cooks, par-cook eggplant slices in small amount of boiling water in a large skillet for about 5 minutes; drain well.

Layer eggplant, Ricotta and Parmesan cheese and tomato sauce in a shallow 8-cup baking dish; ending with a layer of eggplant and sauce, top with Mozzarella cheese.

Bake in a hot oven (425°) for about 15 minutes or until cheese is lightly browned and mixture is bubbly hot.

HAM AND CHEESE QUICHE

Gail Frye

1 (9-inch) pie shell, baked
1 c. shredded Swiss cheese
1 c. chopped ham
6 eggs
1 c. milk
salt and pepper to taste

Sprinkle ham and cheese into pie shell. Beat together remaining ingredients and pour over ham and cheese.

Bake at 375° for 30-40 minutes until a knife inserted into center comes out clean. Let stand 5 minutes before serving.

CHEESEBURGER PIE

Linda Murphy

1 unbaked 9-inch pie crust
1 lb. ground beef
1 tsp. salt
1/2 tsp. oregano
1/4 tsp. pepper
1/2 c. dry bread crumbs
1 (8 oz.) can tomato sauce
1/4 c. chopped onion
1/4 c. chopped green pepper
Cheese Topping (below)
1/2 c. chili sauce

Heat oven to 425°. Prepare pastry for 9-inch (1-crust) pie. In medium skillet, cook and stir meat until brown. Drain off fat. Stir in salt, oregano, pepper, crumbs, 1/2 cup of tomato sauce, the onion and green pepper. Turn into pastry-lined pan.

Spread Cheese Topping over filling. Bake about 30 minutes. Cut into wedges. Stir together remaining tomato sauce and the chili sauce. Serve with pie. 6-8 servings.

Cheese Topping:

1 egg
1/4 c. milk
1/2 tsp. each: salt, dry mustard and Worcestershire sauce
2 c. shredded natural Cheddar cheese (about 8 oz.)

Beat egg and milk; stir in seasonings and cheese.

SQUASH CASSEROLE

Julie Burnham

2 lbs. squash, cut in 1/2-inch slices
3/4 c. chopped onion
3 Tbsp. butter or oil
1 regular block Velveeta mild Mexican, grated
1 block Monterey Jack cheese, grated

Drop squash into boiling water for about 5 minutes. Saute onion lightly in butter. Alternate layers of squash, onions and cheese in a buttered casserole. Finish with cheese.

Bake at 350° for 20 to 30 minutes. Serves 4. Can be doubled.

CHEDDAR CHEESE SOUFFLE

2 Tbsp. butter or margarine
3 Tbsp. all-purpose flour
1 c. milk
3 oz. shredded Cheddar cheese
1/2 tsp. salt
dash cayenne pepper
3 eggs, separated

Place butter in saucepan and melt over medium heat; blend in flour, stirring constantly, add milk and cook until thickened. Remove from heat, stir in cheese, salt and cayenne pepper until smooth. Set aside.

Place egg whites in bowl, beat on high until stiff but not dry. Place egg yolks in a medium-size bowl, beat on high speed for 1 minute. Reduce to low speed, add cheese mixture, beat for 1/2 minute. Very gently fold in firm egg whites. Pour mixture into a greased 1-quart souffle dish.

Bake at 325°F. for 40-45 minutes or until firm.

Yield: 4 servings.

POTATO CASSEROLE

Debbie Caldwell

1-2 (24 oz.) pkg(s). frozen hash browns, partly thawed
1 stick butter, melted
1/2 to 3/4 c. chopped onion or can onion soup
1 pt. sour cream
2 c. grated Cheddar cheese

Break up hash browns into small chunks. Mix all ingredients together in large bowl. Top with Durkee fried onions.

Bake in glass dish at 350° for 45 minutes. Serves 6-8.

CHICKEN AND RICE

Shirley Necessary

1 whole chicken (small)
4 c. cooked rice
2 cans condensed cream of chicken soup
1 tsp. lemon juice
1/2 c. mayonnaise
1/4 tsp. curry powder
1/2 c. shredded cheese (Cheddar), optional
salt and pepper to taste

Cook chicken with lots of water until done (cool and pick off meat). Put cooked rice into casserole dish and chicken.

In a bowl, combine soups, mayonnaise, lemon juice, curry powder. Pour over rice and chicken; mix well. Sprinkle cheese on top and bake 30 minutes or until hot in 350° oven.

HAMBURGER AND MACARONI CASSEROLE
Gail Frye

1/2 lb. mushrooms
1 onion, chopped
1/2 green pepper, chopped
2 Tbsp. oil
1 1/2 lbs. hamburger
1 tsp. salt
1/2 tsp. basil
1/4 tsp. black pepper
1 c. uncooked macaroni
1 small can tomatoes

Cook macaroni and drain. Saute mushrooms, onion and green pepper in oil. Add hamburger and brown. Drain fat. Add remaining ingredients. Put hamburger mixture and cooked macaroni into a baking dish and bake at 350° for 45 minutes.

HOT DOG CASSEROLE
Linda Murphy

1 lb. hot dogs
1/2 c. chopped onion
3 Tbsp. margarine, melted
2 (16 oz.) cans green beans
1 (10 oz.) can condensed tomato soup
6 servings of packaged instant potatoes
1 beaten egg
1/2 c. shredded cheese (optional)

Cook franks and onion in margarine till franks are brown and onion is tender. Stir in green beans and tomato soup. Turn into a 2-quart casserole. Set aside.

Prepare mashed potatoes according to package directions; except reserve milk to make potatoes hold shape. Add egg, beat into potatoes. Mound potatoes on top of frank mixture.

Bake, uncovered at 350° for 25 minutes - top with cheese. Bake till cheese is melted, about 5 minutes.

BAKED SEAFOOD CASSEROLE
Sharon Kline

Serves 8.

1 lb. lump or backfin crabmeat
1 lb. shrimp, steamed, peeled, deveined
1/2 c. finely chopped green pepper
1 c. mayonnaise
1 tsp. Worcestershire sauce
1/4 c. finely chopped (minced) onion
1 c. thinly sliced celery
1/2 tsp. salt
1/4 tsp. pepper

Mix all ingredients together (try to avoid breaking the lumps of crabmeat). Pour into 8 x 8 or equivalent size baking dish. Top with 3/4 cup bread crumbs mixed with 2 tablespoons melted butter. Bake at 350° for 30 minutes.

Note: Recipe can easily be doubled or tripled.

HAMBURGER CASSEROLE

Mrs. Sam Gladwin

6 oz. noodles
1 1/2 lbs. ground beef
2 medium onions, chopped
 or 1 large
1 clove garlic, crushed
2 tsp. flour
1 (15 oz.) can tomatoes, crushed
1/4 c. beef stock
1 Tbsp. soy sauce
1 Tbsp. Worcestershire sauce
1 tsp. oregano

Sauce:

1/2 stick butter
2 Tbsp. flour
1 c. milk
1 1/2 oz. Cheddar cheese

Cook noodles according to directions. Cook beef, add onion, garlic and cook 3-4 minutes. Blend 2 teaspoons flour with some of tomato stock and stir into beef with rest of tomatoes, beef stock, soy sauce, Worcestershire sauce, oregano. Bring to boil and cook 2 minutes, remove from heat.

Cover bottom of casserole dish with small amount of meat mixture - put half noodles in casserole dish, cover with meat mixture, add rest of noodles.

Sauce: Melt butter, stir in flour and cook 1 minute, add milk, stirring continuously, to make a sauce. Pour over noodles, sprinkle cheese over top, cover and cook in oven for 15 minutes.

Uncover and cook 10-15 more minutes. Mushrooms may be added. I sometimes add corn and green peppers. Use your own judgement. Set oven at 350°.

BATTER UP BEEF PIE

Doris Sharp

1/4 c. butter
1 1/2 c. all-purpose flour
2 tsp. baking powder
1 tsp. salt
1 1/2 c. milk
1/2 c. Cheddar cheese, grated
1 (1 1/2 lb.) can Dinty Moore
 beef stew

Melt butter in bottom of 8-inch square baking dish. Combine remaining ingredients, except stew in mixing bowl; stir until blended. Pour over melted butter. Pour beef stew over batter. Do not stir.

Bake at 350° for 60-65 minutes.

CAULIFLOWER CASSEROLE

Mary Parsons

2 (10 oz.) pkgs. frozen cauliflower
1/3 c. all-purpose flour
3 Tbsp. butter or margarine, melted
2 tsp. dried parsley
3 green onions, finely chopped
2 egg yolks
1/2 tsp. salt
dash pepper
1 c. seasoned stuffing

Cook cauliflower according to directions on package until very tender; drain. Place cauliflower and flour in bowl, mix on low speed, 30 seconds. Scrape bowl. Gradually increase speed to medium, beat 1 minute. Scrape bowl. Add 2 tablespoons butter, parsley, onions, egg yolks, salt and pepper. Beat at medium speed for 1 minute.

Place cauliflower mixture into a 3-cup casserole. Mix remaining butter and stuffing together and sprinkle over the casserole. Bake at 400°F. for 20 minutes.

Yield: 4 servings.

MEAT - MACARONI SUPPER

Doris Sharp

2 Tbsp. butter
1/2 c. chopped onion
10 3/4 oz. can cream of celery soup
8 oz. can (1 c.) tomatoes, cut up
1/4 tsp. dried thyme
dash pepper
1 c. macaroni, cooked
1 (12 oz.) can Treet, cut in strips
1/4 c. green peppers
1/4 c. American cheese, shredded

Melt butter in medium skillet and cook onion till tender but not brown. Stir in soup, tomatoes, thyme and pepper. Add cooked macaroni (well drained), strips of Treet and green pepper. Turn in 1 1/2-quart casserole. Top with cheese.

Bake uncovered at 350° for 35-40 minutes. Serves 4-6.

CHICKEN CASSEROLE

Ruth Hale

2 c. diced chicken
1 can cream of celery or mushroom soup
1 c. milk
1 box Stove Top stuffing mix

Butter bottom of casserole dish. Spread chicken in bottom. Pour mixture of soup and milk over chicken. Prepare stuffing mix according to directions. Mound on top of chicken and soup mixture. Bake 15 to 20 minutes until bubbly.

HUNGRY BOYS' CASSEROLE

Linda Murphy

Saute in large skillet:

1 1/2 lbs. ground beef
1 c. sliced celery
1/2 c. chopped onion
1/2 c. chopped green pepper
1 clove garlic, minced

Cook till vegetables are tender. Drain. Add:

3/4 c. (6 oz. can) tomato paste
3/4 c. water
1 tsp. salt
1 tsp. paprika
1/2 tsp. MSG

Reserve 1 cup for biscuits. Add:

1 (1 lb.) can pork and beans
1 (1 lb.) can lima beans

Simmer while preparing biscuits. Sift into bowl:

1 1/2 c. flour
2 tsp. baking powder
1/2 tsp. salt

Cut in 1/4 cup butter. Combine:

1/2 c. milk
4 drops yellow food coloring

Add to flour mixture. Stir till dough clings together. Knead on floured surface 12 times. Roll out to a 12 x 9 rectangle. Spread reserved meat mixture over dough. Roll up, starting with long side, seal edge. Cut into 1-inch pieces.

Put meat into 9 x 13 baking dish; top with biscuits. Bake at 425° for 25-30 minutes until golden brown.

Write an extra recipe here:

VEGETABLES

BUYING GUIDE
Fresh vegetables and fruits

Experience is the best teacher in choosing quality but here are a few pointers on buying some of the fruits and vegetables.

ASPARAGUS—Stalks should be tender and firm, tips should be close and compact. Choose the stalks with very little white—they are more tender. Use asparagus soon—it toughens rapidly.

BEANS, SNAP—Those with small seeds inside the pods are best. Avoid beans with dry-looking pods.

BERRIES—Select plump, solid berries with good color. Avoid stained containers, indicating wet or leaky berries. Berries such as blackberries and raspberries with clinging caps may be underripe. Strawberries without caps may be too ripe.

BROCCOLI, BRUSSELS SPROUTS, AND CAULIFLOWER—Flower clusters on broccoli and cauliflower should be tight and close together. Brussels sprouts should be firm and compact. Smudgy, dirty spots may indicate insects.

CABBAGE AND HEAD LETTUCE—Choose heads heavy for size. Avoid cabbage with worm holes, lettuce with discoloration or soft rot.

CUCUMBERS—Choose long, slender cucumbers for best quality. May be dark or medium green but yellowed ones are undesirable.

MELONS—In cantaloupes, thick close netting on the rind indicates best quality. Cantaloupes are ripe when the stem scar is smooth and space between the netting is yellow or yellow-green. They are best to eat when fully ripe with fruity odor.

Honeydews are ripe when rind has creamy to yellowish color and velvety texture. Immature honeydews are whitish-green.

Ripe watermelons have some yellow color on one side. If melons are white or pale green on one side, they are not ripe.

ORANGES, GRAPEFRUIT, AND LEMONS—Choose those heavy for their size. Smoother, thinner skins usually indicate more juice. Most skin markings do not affect quality. Oranges with a slight greenish tinge may be just as ripe as fully colored ones. Light or greenish-yellow lemons are more tart than deep yellow ones. Avoid citrus fruits showing withered, sunken, or soft areas.

PEAS AND LIMA BEANS—Select pods that are well-filled but not bulging. Avoid dried, spotted, yellowed, or flabby pods.

ROOT VEGETABLES—Should be smooth and firm. Very large carrots may have woody cores, oversized radishes may be pithy, oversized turnips, beets, and parsnips may be woody. Fresh carrot tops usually mean fresh carrots, but condition of leaves on most other root vegetables does not indicate degree of freshness.

SWEET POTATOES—Porto Rico and Nancy Hall varieties—with bronze to rosy skins—are soft and sweet when cooked. Yellow to light-brown ones of the Jersey types are firmer and less moist.

"SWEET" POTATOES

Linda Cole

2-3 large sweet potatoes
1/2 stick margarine or butter
1/4 c. milk
2 c. miniature marshmallows (approximately)

Peel, dice and boil potatoes. Drain and then mash. Add 2 tablespoons margarine, 1/4 cup milk to mashed potatoes and mix until fluffy, salt and pepper to taste.

Spread fluffy mashed potatoes in baking dish evenly. Slice 2 tablespoons of margarine into THIN pats of margarine and place over top of potatoes. Cover potatoes completely with a layer of miniature marshmallows.

Bake at 350° till marshmallows melt, approximately 15 minutes.

CREAMY POTATO CASSEROLE

Morris Family Favorite

8 medium potatoes, peeled and cut into 1-inch cubes
1/3 c. water
8 oz. cream cheese
8 oz. sour cream
1/4 c. chopped chives
1/2 tsp. salt
1/4 tsp. garlic salt
1/2 c. butter or margarine
paprika
fresh parsley

Cook and drain potatoes, mash. Beat cream cheese with electric mixer until smooth. Add potatoes and next 4 ingredients.

Place butter in 1 3/4-quart casserole, microwave till melted. Add potato mixture, combine till thoroughly mixed. Sprinkle with paprika.

Bake 1 hour at 300°.

CORN PUDDING

Misty Frye

1 can creamed corn
1 can whole kernel corn
1 egg
1 Tbsp. flour
salt and pepper to taste
butter

Beat flour and egg together. Mix corns and egg mixture and salt and pepper. Put in casserole pan. Place pats of butter on top of mixture and bake at 325° for 45 minutes.

VEGETABLE-CHEESE QUICHE

Bonnie Carter

- 4 well-beaten eggs (or use equivalent for "Egg Beaters" substitute)
- 2 c. cooked veggies (broccoli, cauliflower or a "medley" of mixed vegetables)
- 1 c. skim milk
- 1 c. grated cheese
- salt and pepper
- 1 Tbsp. parsley
- 1/4 c. grated cheese*
- 1/2 c. crushed cheese crackers*

Combine all ingredients EXCEPT those marked with *'s. Turn into a "Pam"-ed 9-inch pie pan. Bake at 350° for 30 minutes.

Then sprinkle with 1/4 cup grated cheese and cracker crumbs. Bake 5 minutes more or till crumbs start to brown. (Tastes good with Parmesan cheese sprinkled on top also!)

1/4 pie = approximately 250 calories, or: 1 vegetable exchange; 2 meat exchanges; 1/4 milk exchange; 1-2 fat exchanges (depending on which cheeses you use - Cheddar is higher in fat than Swiss, for example. Or you may purchase a low-fat cheese to use).

VEGETABLE CASSEROLE

Linda Laurence

- 1 (16 oz.) bag frozen broccoli, carrots, cauliflower, thawed and drained
- 1 (10 3/4 oz.) can condensed cream of mushroom soup
- 1 c. (4 oz.) shredded Swiss cheese
- 1/3 c. sour cream
- 1/4 tsp. pepper
- 1 (4 oz.) jar chopped pimento, drained
- 1 (2.8 oz.) can French fried onions

Combine vegetables, soup, 1/2 cup cheese, sour cream, pepper, pimento, 1/2 can onions. Pour into 1-quart casserole.

Bake at 350° for 30 minutes. Top with remaining cheese and onions. Bake uncovered 5 minutes longer.

MEXICAN SQUASH CASSEROLE

Julie Burnham

- 2 lbs. squash, cut in 1/2-inch slices
- 3/4 c. chopped onion
- 3 Tbsp. butter or oil
- 2 small blocks mild Mexican Velveeta cheese, sliced
- 1/2 lb. Monterey Jack cheese, grated

Drop squash into boiling water for about 5 minutes. Drain. Saute onion in butter. Alternate layers of squash, onions and cheese in a buttered casserole. Top with a layer of cheese.

Bake at 350° for 20-25 minutes.

ITALIAN ZUCCHINI PIE

Gail Overdest

- 4 c. sliced zucchini
- 1 c. onion, chopped
- 1/2 c. butter
- 1/2 tsp. salt
- 1/2 tsp. pepper
- 1/4 tsp. garlic
- 1/4 tsp. basil
- 1/4 tsp. oregano
- 2 eggs, beaten
- 8 oz. shredded cheese
- 8 oz. can crescent rolls
- 2 tsp. Dijon mustard

(Optional: crispy bacon or Italian sausage.)

Use 9-inch pie pan. Line with crescent rolls. Spread mustard on rolls. Saute first 3 ingredients; add spices and eggs; pour into crust. Add optionals; sprinkle cheese on top.

Bake 20 minutes.

VEGETABLE CHILI

(A "heart-healthy" recipe.)

- 3/4 c. olive oil
- 2 medium zucchini, cut into 1/2-inch cubes
- 2 medium yellow onions, cut into 1/2-inch cubes
- 4 cloves garlic, finely chopped
- 2 large sweet red peppers, cut into 1/4-inch dices
- 1 (35 oz.) can Italian plum tomatoes
- 1 1/2 lbs. fresh ripe plum tomatoes, cut in 1-inch pieces
- 2 tsp. pepper
- 1 tsp. fennel seeds
- 1 Tbsp. ground cumin
- 1 Tbsp. dried oregano
- 1 tsp. salt
- 1/2 c. chopped parsley
- 1 c. canned dark-red kidney beans, drained
- 1 c. canned garbanzos (chick-peas), drained
- 2 Tbsp. lemon juice
- 2 Tbsp. chili powder
- 1 Tbsp. dried basil

In Dutch oven or stew pot, saute zucchini, onions, garlic and red pepper in oil till zucchini is tender (about 10 minutes). Add undrained canned tomatoes, fresh tomatoes and spices. Cook uncovered, stirring often, for 30 minutes.

Stir in beans and lemon juice. Cook 15 minutes. Stir well. To serve, you may want to garnish with low-fat sour cream or grated cheese.

BAKED (PORK AND BEANS)

1 can pork and beans
1 small onion
1 tsp. mustard
1 tsp. brown sugar
salt and pepper to taste
1/2 c. catsup (more if desired)
1 or 2 slices bacon

Mix all together and bake in 375° oven or 400° oven for 30 to 40 minutes.

SKILLET BEANS

1 medium onion
some green pepper
1 can pork and beans

Use as much as you like of season, catsup, salt, pepper and chili powder. Simmer 15 or 20 minutes on low heat.

FRIED RICE

Kris Leonard

1 c. cooked rice
6 Tbsp. vegetable oil
2 eggs, beaten
2 Tbsp. soy sauce
1/4 tsp. Accent
salt to taste
1 small clove garlic
4 green onions
1/2 c. diced meat (chicken, pork, shrimp)

In 10-inch skillet, saute rice over high heat 3-4 minutes. Stir eggs rapidly into rice, cook until set. Reduce heat, add everything else. Heat thoroughly and serve.

BROCCOLI CASSEROLE

Kris Leonard

2 pkgs. frozen chopped broccoli
1 can cream of mushroom soup
2 Tbsp. grated onion
2 beaten eggs
1 c. sharp Cheddar cheese, grated
1 c. Miracle Whip salad dressing

Cook broccoli until tender; drain. Combine soup, onion, eggs, cheese and salad dressing until thoroughly mixed.

Layer broccoli and sauce in greased casserole, add buttered bread crumbs to top.

Bake at 350° for 20-30 minutes. Serves 8.

SAVOURY STIR-FRIED BROCCOLI

Paula McHenry

1/4 c. oil
1/8 tsp. pepper
1/4 c. chopped green onions
1 1/2 tsp. fresh minced garlic
2 c. fresh broccoli, cut in 4-inch pieces
1/4 c. water
1/4 tsp. salt

Heat oil over medium-high heat in large skillet, saute onions and garlic about 1 minute. Add broccoli and cook and stir till coated, about 2 minutes; reduce heat; add water, cover for 5 minutes, remove from heat. Stir-fry another minute, add salt and pepper.

STUFFED BAKED ZUCCHINI

Betty Adelung

2 large zucchini
1/2 lb. cooked ground beef
1 c. canned spaghetti sauce
1 tsp. parsley
1/2 c. Parmesan cheese
1/4 c. chopped onion
1/8 tsp. pepper
1/8 tsp. garlic powder
1/8 tsp. oregano
1/2 c. shredded Mozzarella cheese

Cut zucchini lengthwise and hollow out with a spoon. Mix the pulp with all other ingredients except Mozzarella cheese. Fill hollowed shells with the mixture.

Bake at 350° for about 25 minutes. During last 5 minutes put shredded Mozzarella cheese on top of zucchini and bake until melted.

FRIED RICE

Madeline Nelson
(Kris Miller's Mom)

Makes 4 to 6 servings.

3 strips bacon, diced
3/4 c. chopped green onions and tops
1/3 c. diced red bell pepper (optional)
1/4 c. frozen green peas, thawed
1 egg, beaten
4 c. cooked rice, chilled
2 Tbsp. soy sauce

Cook bacon in wok or large skillet over medium heat until crisp. Add green onions, red pepper and peas. Stir fry 1 minute. Add egg and scramble. Stir in rice and cook until heated, gently separating grains.

Add soy sauce, cook and stir until thoroughly heated. Serve immediately.

SWEET POTATO CASSEROLE — **Debbie Caldwell**

Serves 8.

3 c. cooked sweet potatoes, mashed
1 c. sugar
1/2 tsp. salt
1 Tbsp. cinnamon
1 tsp. nutmeg
2 eggs, beaten
1/2 stick melted butter
1/2 c. evaporated milk
1/2 tsp. vanilla

Combine all ingredients above, mix and pour into casserole dish.

Topping:

1 c. brown sugar
1/3 c. flour
1 c. nuts, chopped
1/3 stick melted butter

Combine topping ingredients. Place mixture over sweet potatoes. Bake at 350° for approximately 40 minutes.

BROCCOLI AND MUSHROOM CHEESE MELT

Mary Parsons

1 lb. broccoli (fresh or frozen)
1 (8 oz.) can sliced mushrooms
6-8 oz. shredded Mozzarella cheese

Cook broccoli and drain. In a shallow baking pan arrange broccoli in a single layer. Drain mushrooms and spread over broccoli. Cover vegetables with cheese.

Place in 350° oven for 10 minutes, until cheese has evenly melted over vegetables. Serves 4-6.

FRIED RICE — **Portia Mae Morris**

1/4 c. plus 2 Tbsp. butter
2 eggs, beaten
2/3 c. chopped green onions
2/3 c. chopped sweet red peppers
2 2/3 c. cooked rice
2/3 c. water
1 c. cooked peas
1/4 c. soy sauce

Melt butter in a skillet, add eggs, cook over medium heat until almost set. Stir in next 3 ingredients; cook, stirring frequently, about 5 minutes or until lightly browned. Add water and soy sauce. Cook 2 minutes.

Yield: 8 servings.

MY FAVORITE SPINACH PIE/SPANAKOPITA

Portia Mae Morris

2 (10 oz.) pkgs. frozen chopped spinach
2 c. cottage cheese
1 2/3 c. crumbled Feta cheese
3 eggs, beaten
4 green onions with tops, chopped
1/4 tsp. dried whole dill weed
1 tsp. oregano
1/2 tsp. pepper
1/4 tsp. dried whole thyme
1 (1 lb.) pkg. frozen phyllo pastry, thawed
1 c. butter, melted

Cook spinach according to package directions - omitting salt. Drain well and press in paper towels till barely moist.

Combine spinach, cottage cheese, Feta cheese, eggs, green onions, dill weed, oregano, pepper and thyme. Mix well, set aside.

Cut phyllo sheets in half crosswise to fit 13 x 9 x 2 inch baking pan. Cover with a slightly damp towel. Lightly butter bottom and sides of pan, layer 1/2 phyllo sheets in pan, brushing each sheet with melted butter. (Keep remaining sheets cover with damp towel.)

Spread spinach mixture evenly over phyllo in pan. Top with remaining phyllo, brushing each sheet with remaining butter. Bake at 350° for 40 to 45 minutes or until golden brown.

Yield: 8 servings.

CORN PUDDING

Portia Mae Morris

2 c. corn
2 eggs, slightly beaten
3/4 c. milk
2 Tbsp. sugar
2 Tbsp. diced onion
2 Tbsp. butter or margarine, melted
1/2 tsp. salt
1/8 tsp. pepper

Combine all ingredients; mix well. Pour into a lightly greased 1-quart baking dish. Bake uncovered at 350° for 30 minutes or until firm.

ETHEL MORRIS'S GREEN BEANS

Ethel Morris

1/4 lb. fat back
1 tsp. pepper
3 qts. green beans (fresh beans are best)

In large pot, simmer fat back till brown, add beans and cover with water. Cook over medium heat till beans are cooked. Remove fat back before serving. (Beans are usually done when most of liquid is gone.)

THOMAS JEFFERSON STEWED TOMATOES

Ethel Morris

2 large cans stewed tomatoes
3 large buttermilk biscuits
3 Tbsp. sugar
1 tsp. pepper

Empty stewed tomatoes into large saucepan, break up biscuits in small pieces. Add sugar and heat through before serving in small saucers.

BROCCOLI/CAULIFLOWER SALAD

Lola Haley

1 lb. bacon
1 head broccoli
1 head cauliflower
1 red onion
1/4 c. sugar
1/3 c. vinegar
1 c. mayonnaise

Cook bacon and crumble. Chop broccoli and cauliflower into small pieces, finely chop onion. Mix sugar, vinegar and mayonnaise (a blender works well). Combine all ingredients and refrigerate at least 8 hours.

SHIRLEY TEMPLE'S BAKED PINEAPPLE

Shirley Sadler
Pastor Morris' Cousin

1 (No. 10) can crushed pineapple
1 stick butter
6 slices bread (white)
1 1/2 c. sugar
1 egg

Melt butter in heavy skillet, add crumbed bread, slightly beaten egg. Add pineapple and sugar, mix in bread crumbs and butter.

Bake in 2-quart dish for 30 minutes at 350°.

SWEET POTATO CASSEROLE

Portia Mae Morris

3 c. cooked, mashed sweet potatoes
3/4 c. sugar
2 eggs
1 tsp. vanilla
1/2 c. water

Combine all ingredients above. Add topping:

1 c. brown sugar
1/3 c. flour
1 1/2 c. coarsely chopped pecans
1/3 c. soft butter

Spread on top. Bake at 350° for 30 minutes.

TWICE BAKED POTATOES AND TOPPERS
Mary Parsons

5 large baked potatoes
1/2 c. milk, heated
3 Tbsp. butter or margarine
salt and pepper

Cut potatoes in half and scoop out interior, leaving skin shell intact, set shells aside.

Place scooped out potato in warmed bowl, beat at medium speed for 1 minute. Add milk, margarine, salt and pepper. Gradually turn to medium speed, beat until milk is absorbed, about 30 seconds. Gradually increase to high speed and beat until fluffy, about 1 minute. Fill shells with potatoes and top.

Potato Toppers:

1: Mushroom and Onions:

Saute mushrooms and onions in margarine until tender. Spoon over potato and bake at 350° for 10-15 minutes or until heated through.

2: Bacon and Cheddar:

Sprinkle bacon bits and Cheddar cheese over potatoes. Place under broiler until cheese is melted and potatoes are heated through.

PENNSYLVANIA FARM CORN PUDDING
Portia Mae Morris

1 (No. 1) can cream-style corn
1 c. milk
1 can regular corn
1 c. medium fine dry bread crumbs
2 Tbsp. chopped green pepper
1/4 tsp. pepper
4 oz. Cheddar cheese, cut in 1 1/2-inch squares
3 slices bacon, cut in 1 1/2-inch lengths

Combine corn, crumbs, milk, green pepper, pepper in 10 x 6 x 2-inch baking dish.

Arrange alternate pieces of cheese and bacon on top (checkerboard fashion).

Bake at 325° for 1 1/4 hours.

SPINACH CASSEROLE **Barbara Shenahan**

2 pkgs. frozen chopped spinach
1 packet Lipton onion soup mix
1 pt. sour cream
1 stick butter/margarine
1/2 (7 oz.) pkg. Pepperidge Farm seasoned stuffing

Cook spinach until done and drain well. Put into 2-quart baking dish. Add margarine and sour cream and stir until well blended. Add soup mix and stuffing.

Bake at 350° for 25 minutes.

(Chopped broccoli may be used instead of spinach.)

Write your extra recipes here:

BREAD ROLLS
PIES • PASTRY

BREAD, ROLLS, PIES AND PASTRY

* Place a folded, damp towel under the bowl and it won't slip and slide while mixing.

* When fresh fruit is handy, but you don't have time to bake, just mix the filling as you normally would for pie. Line a pie pan with several layers of foil and place the filling in the pan. Wrap and freeze. When you're ready with a pie crust the filling can be placed in the crust and baked. After filling is frozen solid it can be taken out of the pan so you will be able to use the pan and the fillings will stack neater in the freezer.

* Add ½ teaspoon of sugar to the yeast when stirring it into the water to dissolve. If it foams and bubbles in ten minutes you know the yeast is alive and active.

* Dough can rise with no problem even in a cold kitchen if the bowl is placed on a heating pad set on medium.

* If the oven is turned off just when the meringue is brown, and the door is left slightly open, the pie cools slowly and prevents the meringue from splitting.

* Your bread will be crusty if top and sides are brushed with an egg white that has been beaten with one tablespoon of water.

* A super-fast 'company' pie can be made by using a prepared crust. Add one box of instant pudding mix to prepared whipped topping. Mix well and fill crust. Reserve enough whipped topping to cover pie. Any flavor pudding mix can be used.

* Try substituting ground nuts in a one crust pie. Press pie shell just like you would with a graham cracker crust.

* Use water that has been used to boil potatoes to make bread dough moister.

* If a dull-finish aluminum loaf pan is used it will brown the sides of the bread better.

* Brushing frozen pies with melted butter before baking can eliminate dryness.

* Let baked bread cool on a wire rack so the bottom won't be soggy.

* Dough won't stick to your hands if it is kneaded inside a large plastic bag.

* Using lard instead of shortening will yield a much flakier crust.

* To get a dull finish on a new pan it can be baked empty in a 350 degree oven.

* If the television is in use, it makes a nice warm spot for dough to rise.

APPLESAUCE BREAD PUDDING

Bonnie Swecker

4 slices toasted white bread
1/3 c. raisins
2 eggs
1/4 c. sugar
1 (16 1/2 oz.) can Musselman applesauce
2 Tbsp. butter or margarine
1/2 c. Pet evaporated milk
1 tsp. vanilla
4 tsp. sugar
1/4 tsp. cinnamon

Spread toasted bread with butter and cut into quarters.

Place buttered side up in greased 1 1/2-quart baking dish. Sprinkle raisins over toast.

Mix eggs, sugar, applesauce, milk and vanilla and pour over toast. Let stand 10 minutes.

Sprinkle sugar and cinnamon over top and bake in 350° oven 35 minutes or until knife inserted near edge comes out clean. Serve warm or cold.

Makes 4 servings.

PINEAPPLE BRAN MUFFINS

Bran muffin mix from Price Club, substitute 1 cup pineapple juice for water. (1 can pineapple chunks (shredded) = water.)

1 banana, chopped
1 1/2 c. pecans or walnuts

Mix together and bake in greased and well-floured muffin tins. Bake at 325° for 25 minutes or till pick in center comes out clean.

CHRIS'S APPLE CRUMB PIE - 1978

Portia Morris

5-7 tart apples (5 c.)
1 (9-inch) unbaked pastry shell
1/2 c. sugar
3/4 tsp. ground cinnamon
1/3 c. sugar
3/4 c. all-purpose flour
6 Tbsp. butter

Pare, core and cut apples in eighths. Arrange in unbaked pastry shell. Mix 1/2 cup sugar and cinnamon; sprinkle over apples. Mix 1/3 cup sugar with flour; cut in butter until crumbly. Sprinkle over apples.

Bake at 400° for 35-40 minutes or till done.

CRANBERRY MINCE PIE

Bonnie Swecker

Makes 9- or 10-inch pie.

2/3 c. sugar
2 Tbsp. cornstarch
2/3 c. water
1 1/2 c. fresh cranberries, rinsed and drained*
pastry for 2-pie crusted
1 jar Non Such ready-to-use mincemeat
1 egg yolk, plus 2 Tbsp. water mixed

*You can use whole canned cranberries, if desired.

In saucepan, combine sugar and cornstarch, add water. Over high heat, cook and stir until boiling. Add cranberries, return to a boil, reduce heat, simmer 5 to 10 minutes, stirring occasionally.

Put mincemeat into pastry-lined 9- or 10-inch pie plate. Top with cranberries. Cover with vented top crust. Seal and flute. Brush egg mixture over crust.

Bake at 425° for 30 minutes or until brown.

Egg Nog Cream Topping for Pie:

In large bowl, combine:

1 1/2 c. canned Borden egg nog, chilled
1 (4 serving size) pkg. instant vanilla pudding

Mix well. Fold in 1/2 pint Borden whipped cream, whipped. Use for topping for pie, cakes or fruit.

Makes 3 1/2 cups.

APPLE CUSTARD TART

Linda Cole

9- to 10-inch unbaked pastry shell
1 1/2 c. sour cream
1 (14 oz.) can sweetened condensed milk
1/4 c. frozen concentrated apple juice
1 egg
1 1/2 tsp. vanilla extract
1/4 tsp. cinnamon
2 medium apples, peeled, cored, thinly sliced (approximately 2 c.)
1 Tbsp. margarine

Apple/Cinnamon Glaze:

1/4 frozen juice
1/4 tsp. cornstarch
1/4 tsp. cinnamon

Glaze: Combine in saucepan. Cook over low heat till thickened.

Heat oven to 375°. Bake shell for 15 minutes.

In regular-size bowl, mix cream, milk, juice, egg, vanilla and cinnamon; mix completely. Pour into pie shell.

Bake 30 minutes or until set. Cool. Cook apples till tender-crisp. Spread over cooled pie. Sprinkle with glaze.

EASY REFRIGERATOR ROLLS

Debbie Caldwell

*No kneading - fresh rolls every day.

2 c. warm water (not hot - 110° to 115°)
2 pkgs. active dry yeast
1/2 c. sugar
2 tsp. salt
1/4 c. soft shortening (Crisco)
1 egg
6 1/2- 7 c. flour

Dissolve yeast in water; stir in sugar, salt, shortening and egg.

Mix in flour with hand until dough is easy to handle. Put in greased bowl, cover with damp cloth; place in refrigerator.

About 2 hours before baking, shape dough into rolls (2-3 small balls) and place in greased pans. (Can use cupcake pans.)

Cover and let rise until double in size, 1 1/2-2 hours.

Preheat oven to 400°. Bake 12-15 minutes. Makes approximately 4 dozen medium rolls.

Dough will keep 5 days in refrigerator. Punch down dough if it starts to rise.

SAVORY DRESSING OR STUFFING

Debbie Caldwell

4-5 medium potatoes
1 pkg. Pepperidge Farm herb flavored bread crumbs
3 onions, chopped
2 cans chicken broth
1 stick margarine or butter, melted
spices: savory, thyme
1 c. chopped celery

Cook potatoes, mash, then add rest of ingredients. Add spices to suit your taste. (Savory is strong; go easy.)

Mix ingredients together till well moistened. Bake with turkey or chicken.

WHITE BREAD

Madeline Nelson
(Kris Miller's Mom)

2 pkgs. active dry yeast
3/4 c. warm water (105° to 115°)
2 2/3 c. warm water
1/3 c. sugar
1 Tbsp. salt
3 Tbsp. shortening
9 to 10 c. flour
soft margarine or butter

Dissolve yeast in 3/4 cup warm water. Stir in 2 2/3 cups warm water, sugar, salt, shortening and 5 cups of flour. Beat until smooth. Mix in enough remaining flour to make dough easy to handle. Turn dough onto lightly floured board; knead until smooth and elastic, about 10 minutes.

Place in greased bowl; turn greased side up. Cover; let rise in warm place until double, about 1 hour.

Punch down dough; divide in 1/2. Roll each 1/2 into rectangle 18 x 9 inches. Roll up, beginning at short side. With side of hand press each end to seal. Fold ends under loaf. Place seam side down in greased loaf pan, 9 x 5 x 3 inches. Brush loaves lightly with butter. Let rise until double, about 1 hour.

Heat oven to 425°. Bake 30 to 35 minutes. Remove from pans, brush loaves with soft butter. Cool on wire rack.

PINEAPPLE MUFFINS

Kathy Letson

About 1 dozen.

1 (8 1/2 oz.) can crushed pineapple
3/4 c. milk
1 egg, slightly beaten
1 1/2 tsp. grated orange rind
2 c. sifted all-purpose flour
2 c. sugar
1 Tbsp. baking powder
1/4 tsp. salt
1/4 tsp. nutmeg
1/4 c. melted butter

1. Drain pineapple liquid into a measuring cup. Add enough milk to make 1 cup. Combine with egg and orange rind.

2. In separate bowl, sift together flour, sugar, baking powder, salt and nutmeg.

3. Blend milk mixture into dry ingredients, along with the melted butter, mixing just until batter is blended. Stir in crushed pineapple.

4. Spoon into lightly buttered muffin pans. Bake at 400°F. for 20 minutes, or until golden and set. Cool slightly. Then remove from pan and serve warm.

PUMPKIN CHIFFON PIE

Joye Moody

3 eggs, separated
1 c. sugar
1 1/4 c. pumpkin
1/4 c. milk
1/4 c. sherry
1/2 tsp. salt
1/2 tsp. nutmeg
1/2 tsp. cinnamon
1 envelope gelatin
1/4 c. cold water
1 baked pie shell
whipped cream

Combine slightly beaten egg yolks, pumpkin, 1/2 cup sugar, milk, sherry, salt and spices; cook in double boiler until thickened. Soften gelatin in cold water for 5 minutes, add to pumpkin mixture, stir until dissolved. Cool until it begins to thicken.

Beat egg whites until stiff, gradually add 1/2 cup sugar, fold into pumpkin. Pour into pie shell. Chill, top with whipped cream.

CARROT AND RAISIN MUFFINS

Paula Scheerer

2 c. flour
1/2 c. sugar
1/2 tsp. salt
1 c. shredded carrots
1/2 c. raisins
3 tsp. baking powder
1/4 c. shortening
1 egg
3/4 c. milk

Mix flour, sugar, salt like for a pie. Then add egg, beaten up and add carrots, milk, baking powder.

Bake at 375° for 25 minutes.

AUNT DORRIS' QUICK BISCUITS

Bonnie's

Combine the following:

1 c. self-rising flour
2 Tbsp. mayonnaise
1/2 c. milk

Bake in greased muffin tins at 425° until brown.
Makes about 8.

DOG BISCUITS

Thought someone might get a kick out of this one!

1/2 c. powdered milk
1 egg, beaten
2 1/2 c. flour
1/2 tsp. salt
1 tsp. brown sugar
1/2 c. cold water
6 Tbsp. meat drippings or butter

Roll to 1/2-inch thickness on lightly oiled cookie sheet. Cut biscuits with cutter. Bake 25-30 minutes at 350°.

GINGERBREAD WAFFLES

Bonnie's

3 eggs
1/4 c. sugar
1/2 c. molasses
1 c. sour milk
1 1/2 c. flour
1 tsp. ginger
1/2 tsp. salt
1 tsp. soda
1 tsp. baking powder
1/3 c. melted shortening

Beat eggs until light. Add sugar and molasses and sour milk to mixture. Sift together dry ingredients and add to mixture. Stir until smooth. Add shortening. Bake. Serve with butter and confectioner's sugar.

CHEOREG (ARMENIAN ROLLS)

Portia Morris

1/2 c. sugar
3/4 c. melted butter
1 1/2 tsp. baking powder
1 tsp. salt
3 eggs, beaten
1 1/2 c. lukewarm milk
2 yeast cakes (or pkgs.)
5 1/2 c. sifted flour (will use more while kneading)
2 egg whites, slightly beaten

Mix together in large bowl until smooth, the sugar, melted butter, baking powder, salt and eggs. Stir in lukewarm milk. Crumble or pour (depends on type of yeast used) yeast into this mixture - 2 yeast cakes and stir until dissolved. Mix in 5 1/2 cups sifted flour gradually, first with spoon, then by hand*, and knead until well blended (about 2 or 3 minutes), scraping all dough from sides of bowl.

*(I put mine on a board, added more flour and kneaded as dough was too mushy.)

Cover and let rise in a warm place until double in bulk (1 1/2 hours approximately). Punch down dough, break off pieces about the size of an egg and shape into desired forms (crescents, braids, rounds, twists) and place on ungreased baking sheets. Brush with slightly beaten egg whites and let rise in a warm place until double - 30 minutes approximately. Bake in 375° oven for 10 to 15 minutes or until delicately brown. (Sesame seeds can be patted on with fingers after applying egg whites.)

Note: I place this recipe in memory of my BEST CHILDHOOD FRIEND, **Lorna Messerlian,** who died with cancer at age 39. Lorna, an Armenian, loved to eat (anything) and many happy memories were made as we embarked on restaurant tours together. I know she loved these rolls more than money and I loved her best!

BANANA NUT BREAD

Mary Parsons

1/3 c. shortening
1/2 c. sugar
2 eggs
1 3/4 c. sifted all-purpose flour
1 tsp. baking powder
1/2 tsp. baking soda
1/2 tsp. salt
1 c. mashed ripe bananas
1/2 c. chopped walnuts

Mix shortening and sugar on high speed for 1 minute, scrape bowl. Add eggs, beat on medium speed for 30 seconds, then on high for 1-2 minutes.

Sift together flour, baking powder, soda and salt in separate bowl. Stir 1/2 of flour mixture and 1/2 of bananas into sugar, shortening and egg mixture. Mix for 1 minute. Add remaining bananas and flour mixture, mix 1 more minute. Fold in walnuts.

Pour mixture into greased and floured 9 1/2 x 5 x 3-inch loaf pan. Bake at 350°F. for 40-45 minutes. Remove from pan and cool on rack.

SWEDISH APPLE PIE

Betty Lou Schere

4 apples
1 Tbsp. sugar
1 tsp. cinnamon
3/4 c. melted butter or margarine
3/4 c. sugar
1 egg, unbeaten
pinch salt
1 c. flour
1/4 c. chopped nuts

Grease 9-inch pie pan. Fill with apples (sliced). Sprinkle with 1 tablespoon sugar and 1 teaspoon cinnamon (mixed together).

Mix melted butter, 3/4 cup sugar, egg, salt. Add flour and nuts. Pour over apples.

Bake at 350° for 45 minutes.

FREEZER WHOLE WHEAT BREAD

Kathy Letson

Three loaves at a time. Very special.

1 c. milk
1/2 c. firmly-packed light brown sugar
1/4 c. granulated sugar
2 Tbsp. salt
1/2 c. (1 stick) butter
2 1/4 c. warm water (105°-115°)
3 pkgs. active dry yeast
3 c. unsifted whole wheat flour
7-8 c. unsifted white flour
melted butter

Scald milk; stir in brown sugar, granulated sugar, salt and 1/2 cup butter. Stir until butter melts. Cool to lukewarm. Measure warm water into large bowl. Sprinkle in yeast; stir until dissolved. Add lukewarm milk mixture, whole wheat flour and 1 cup white flour; beat until smooth. Stir in enough additional white flour to make a stiff dough.

Turn out onto lightly floured board; knead until smooth and elastic, about 12 minutes. Cover; let rest on board 15 minutes. Roll dough out into 18 x 12-inch rectangle. Cut into 3 equal pieces, 6 x 12 inches each. Brush with melted butter.

Stack dough on a greased baking sheet, brushed side up, placing plastic wrap between each piece. Cover sheet tightly with plastic wrap; place in freezer. When frozen, separate pieces of dough and wrap each with plastic wrap. Keep frozen up to 4 weeks.

Remove from freezer. Unwrap and place on ungreased baking sheets, brushed side up. Cover; let stand at room temperature until fully thawed, about 2 1/2 hours. Roll each piece to an 8 x 12-inch rectangle. Beginning at an 8-inch end, roll dough as for jelly roll. Pinch seams to seal. With seam side down, press down ends with heel of hand. Fold underneath. Place each, seam side down, in a greased 8 1/2 x 4 1/2-inch loaf pan. Cover; let rise in warm place, free from draft, until doubled in bulk, about 2 hours and 15 minutes.

Bake on lowest rack position at 375° about 35 minutes, or until done. Remove from pans; cool on racks. Makes 3 loaves.

To bake without freezing: After shaping, let rise in warm place, free from draft, until doubled in bulk. (Unfrozen dough will rise faster than frozen dough.)

MONKEY BREAD

Frances Powers

4 cans Pillsbury buttermilk biscuits (10 biscuits/can)
1 c. brown sugar
2 tsp. cinnamon
1 c. white granulated sugar
2 sticks butter or margarine

Grease bundt pan, cut biscuits into quarters. Mix brown sugar and cinnamon together. Roll biscuits in mix. Line biscuits in pan, layering as you build it up in the pan (biscuits, then sugar mixture, then biscuits, etc.)

Melt 2 sticks butter, add 1 cup sugar - bring to a full rolling boil. Pour over all biscuits.

Bake at 350° for 45 minutes. Turn out on aluminum foil immediately. Take running syrup from around bread and baste over the top. Let cool.

Raisins and nuts may be added as you layer the biscuits in the bundt pan.

SUGARLESS STRAWBERRY PIE

Kris Leonard

5 c. strawberries
3 Tbsp. cornstarch
1/2 c. honey
1/2 c. boiling water
3 tsp. lemon juice
pie crust for 1 (8- or 9-inch) pie, baked

Mash some berries to make 1 cup. Place cornstarch, crushed berries and honey in small saucepan. Add boiling water and cook over medium heat until thickened and clear. Be sure to stir frequently.

Remove from heat and add lemon juice. Place whole berries in pie crust and pour cooled sauce over them. Make sure berries are completely coated. Chill and serve.

BLENDER COCONUT PIE

Mrs. Sam Gladwin

2 c. milk or buttermilk
4 eggs
1/2 c. sugar
1 c. flaked coconut
1/2 c. Bisquick
1 tsp. vanilla
1/4 c. margarine
1/2 tsp. salt

Blend all ingredients in blender at high speed 2 minutes. Pour into greased and floured 9-inch pie pan.

Bake at 350° for 45 minutes. Let cool.

CHEDDAR CHEESE LOAF

Mary Parsons

1 3/4 c. milk
1/2 c. water
3 Tbsp. butter or margarine
6 1/2-7 1/2 c. all-purpose flour
2 Tbsp. sugar
1 Tbsp. salt
2 pkgs. active dry yeast
2 c. shredded sharp Cheddar cheese
2 Tbsp. butter or margarine, melted

Combine milk, water and 3 tablespoons butter in saucepan. Heat over low heat until very warm (120°-130°), set aside.

Place 6 cups flour in large bowl, add sugar, salt and yeast. Mix together. Continue mixing while gradually adding cheese, then warm liquid. Continue to add remaining flour, 1/2 cup at a time, until dough clings to beaters and cleans sides of bowl.

Knead for 5 minutes until dough is smooth and elastic. Place in greased bowl, turn to grease top. Cover, let rise in warm place, free from draft, until doubled in bulk, about 45 minutes.

Punch dough down. Divide into 32 equal pieces. Shape each piece into a smooth ball. Arrange 16 balls in bottom of greased 10-inch tube pan. Brush with melted butter. Arrange remaining 16 balls of dough on top. Brush with melted butter. Cover; let rise in warm place, free from draft, until doubled in bulk, about 45 minutes.

Bake at 375° for 40 minutes or until done. Remove from pan and cool on wire rack.

BUBBLE LOAF

Sherry Heward

1 pkg. active dry yeast
1/3 c. warm water
1 c. milk, scalded
1 Tbsp. sugar
1 Tbsp. butter or margarine
2 tsp. salt
4 c. all-purpose flour
melted butter

1. Combine yeast and warm water in large bowl. Let stand 5 minutes.

2. In saucepan, combine milk, sugar, butter and salt. Heat until butter melts. Stir into yeast mixture.

3. Add 1 cup of the flour. Beat until dough is elastic. Gradually stir in about 2 1/2 cups more flour or until a stiff dough is formed.

4. On lightly floured surface, knead dough for 15 minutes. Place in greased bowl, turning once. Cover and let rise 1 hour in warm place until doubled.

5. Punch down. Divide dough in half. Cut 1 half into 8 pieces. Shape each piece into a ball. Dip each ball into melted butter. Place balls side by side in 2 rows in greased 9 by 5-inch loaf pan. Repeat with remaining dough in another loaf pan.

6. Cover and let rise in warm place 45 minutes longer.

7. Bake at 350° for 45 to 55 minutes or until golden brown. Remove from pan. Cool on rack.

MISSISSIPPI MUD PIE

Kris Miller

- fudge sauce (Evans or other brand)
- 1 packaged chocolate crumb crust
- 1 Tbsp. instant coffee
- 3 1/2 c. (8 oz.) Cool Whip
- 1 pkg. Jell-O vanilla instant pudding
- 1 1/2 c. cold half & half, light cream or milk

Pour half & half into large mixing bowl. Add pie filling mix and instant coffee. Beat 1 minute with wire whisk. Let stand 5 minutes.

Fold in whipped topping. Spoon into crust. Freeze until firm, about 6 hours.

To serve, remove from freezer, let stand 10 minutes to soften. Top with fudge sauce. Store in freezer until ready to use.

BREAD PUDDING

Madeline Nelson
(Kris Miller's Mom)

- 1 c. sugar
- 3/4 c. brown sugar
- 1/2 tsp. salt
- 3 c. milk
- 1/2 c. margarine
- 1 tsp. cinnamon
- 4 eggs
- 1 tsp. vanilla extract
- 1 loaf bread, torn into small pieces

Mix sugars, salt, margarine, cinnamon, eggs and vanilla extract. Scald milk. Add to dry mixture, stirring slowly and constantly until mixed. Add bread and raisins.

Put in greased pan and bake at 350° for 45 to 55 minutes. Test by inserting knife. If it comes out clean it is done.

ENGLISH SCONES **Kathy Letson**

Afternoon tea. Makes 18 scones.

No special tea party would be complete without warm scones like these, which are filled with currants. Serve them hot from the oven with honey, assorted jams, curls of sweet butter, and a bowl of unsweetened whipped cream.

3 3/4 c. all-purpose flour
2 1/2 tsp. baking powder
1/2 c. granulated sugar
1/2 tsp. baking soda
1 tsp. salt
3/4 c. unsalted butter
3/4 c. currants
grated rind from 1 orange
1 c. buttermilk
1/4 c. half & half

In a deep pottery bowl, combine the flour, baking powder, sugar, soda and salt. Using a pastry blender, cut the butter into the flour mixture until it resembles coarse meal. Add currants and orange rind.

Gradually add buttermilk, and mix just until dough combines and holds. Do not overmix. Turn the dough out onto a lightly floured cloth-covered board. Pat or gently roll dough into a 1/2-inch thick round and cut out scones using a 2-inch biscuit cutter or an inverted glass dipped in flour. Brush top of scones with the half & half before baking.

Place on a very lightly greased baking sheet. Bake in preheated 450° oven for about 10 minutes, or until golden brown and puffed. Serve at once.

PUMPKIN ROLL **Becky Marcucci**

3 eggs
1 c. sugar
2/3 c. pumpkin
1 tsp. salt
1 tsp. baking soda
1/2 tsp. cinnamon
3/4 c. flour

Filling:

1 (8 oz.) cream cheese
1 tsp. vanilla
2 Tbsp. soft oleo
1 c. powdered sugar

Preheat oven to 350°. Mix first 7 ingredients. Bake on greased and floured cookie sheet for approximately 15 minutes.

Sprinkle tea towel with powdered sugar. Roll cake in tea towel and let cool for 45 minutes.

Mix filling ingredients. Unroll cake and spread with filling. Nuts may be added to filling.

KEY LIME PIE — Mary Parsons

1 (3 oz.) pkg. lime flavor gelatin
1 c. boiling water
1-2 tsp. grated lime rind
1/2 c. lime juice
1 egg yolk, well beaten
1 (14 oz.) can sweetened condensed milk (1 1/2 c.)
1 egg white
few drops green food coloring (optional)
1 baked 9-inch pie shell, cooled

Dissolve gelatin in boiling water. Add lime rind and juice and pour slowly into beaten egg yolk, stirring constantly.

Add condensed milk and chill until slightly thickened.

Beat egg white until stiff peaks will form; fold into gelatin mixture. Add food coloring. Pour into pie shell. Chill until firm, about 3 hours.

Garnish with whipped topping and lime slices, if desired.

SWEET DOUGH — Mary Parsons

3/4 c. milk
1/2 c. sugar
1 1/4 tsp. salt
1/2 c. butter or margarine
1/3 c. warm water (105°-115°F.)
3 eggs, room temperature
2 pkgs. active dry yeast
5 1/2-6 1/2 c. all-purpose flour

Scald milk; stir in sugar, salt and butter. Cool to lukewarm (115°F.). Pour warm water into warmed bowl. Add yeast and stir until dissolved. Add lukewarm milk mixture, eggs and 5 cups flour. Stir. Place ball on floured counter top, knead for 5 to 10 minutes, adding flour, 1/2 cup at a time. Knead until dough is smooth and elastic. (This can be done in a mixer if you have a dough hook.)

Place dough in greased bowl, turning to grease top. Cover; let rise in warm place, free from draft, until doubled in bulk, about 1 hour.

Punch dough down and shape as desired for rolls or coffee cakes.

NUT BREAD — Frances Marsh

1 egg
1/2 c. brown sugar
1/2 tsp. salt

Beat until smooth. Add:

1 1/2 c. milk
4 c. flour
4 tsp. baking powder
1 c. chopped English walnuts

Put into pan, let rise 1/2 hour. Bake in slow oven for 3/4 hour.

CINNAMON BUNS

Mary Parsons

1 c. brown sugar
1 c. sugar
1/2 c. butter or margarine
1/4 c. all-purpose flour
1 1/2 Tbsp. cinnamon
1/2 c. chopped nuts (optional)
1 recipe Sweet Dough (see page 73)

Mix brown sugar, sugar, margarine, flour, cinnamon and nuts in bowl on medium speed for a minute or so.

Roll dough to a 10 x 30-inch rectangle, 1/4 thick. Spread sugar-cinnamon mixture evenly on dough. Roll dough tightly from long side to form 30-inch roll, pinch seams together. Cut into inch and 1/2 slices. Place 7 rolls in each greased 8-inch round cake pan. Cover; let rise in warm place, free of draft, until doubled in bulk, about 1 hour.

Bake at 350°F. for about 20 minutes. Remove from pans immediately. Spread caramel glaze over warm rolls.

MA'S ROLLY POLY'S

Portia Mae Morris

cinnamon
sugar
butter, softened
pie dough for 2-crust pie

Mix cinnamon and sugar to suit your personal taste. Roll out pie dough into large rectangle. Spread butter over entire area. Sprinkle cinnamon and sugar mixture evenly covering all but the long end closest to you. Begin rolling (long side first) away from you. Cut roll in 1-inch increments.

Bake at 350° for 30 minutes or until golden brown.

Write an extra recipe here:

CAKES • ICINGS
COOKIES

CAKES, ICINGS AND COOKIES

* Adding a pinch of baking powder to powdered sugar icing will help it stay moist and not crack.

* Your frosting will look more professional if you first frost with a thin layer and let it set. Then apply a second coat of frosting.

* An easy way to form drop cookies is to drop them onto the cookie sheet and then press them with the bottom of a water glass that has been dipped in sugar.

* To preserve the creamy texture of frozen cheesecake, thaw in refrigerator for 12 hours.

* Dipping the cookie cutter in slightly warm salad oil will give you a much cleaner cut.

* A quick frosting can be made by adding a bit of chocolate syrup to prepared whipped topping.

* If powdered sugar is sprinkled on top of each layer before filling or frosting, this will keep the filling from soaking through the cake.

* Spaghetti is great with cake! While waiting for icing to set, a few sticks of dry spaghetti will hold the layers in place. Also, a piece of raw spaghetti works well to light birthday candles.

* To cut down on cholesterol, substitute two egg whites stiffly beaten for each whole egg called for.

* Icings won't become grainy if a pinch of salt is added to the sugar.

* Use cocoa to dust baking tins so cookies and cakes won't have a floury look.

* Trace the bottom of the baking pan onto wax paper and cut it out. Now this can be placed in the bottom of the pan and the sides greased and floured like normal. When the cake is done it can be inverted and the paper taken off while still warm with no sticking.

* For a thinner, crispier rolled cookie try rolling the dough directly onto a greased and floured cookie sheet. Cut the cookies out then pick up the scrap dough.

* If eggs are beaten and added slowly to batter it won't make the batter too stiff.

* Cookies will stay moist in the jar if a slice of bread is placed in the jar.

* Two tablespoons of salad oil added to cake mix keeps the mix moist, less crumbly.

* Adding a pinch of salt to chocolate dishes will enhance the flavor.

PUMPKIN CAKE — **Bonnie Swecker**

2 c. pumpkin
1 c. vegetable oil
2 c. sugar
4 eggs, beaten
2 c. flour
2 tsp. baking soda
2 tsp. cinnamon
1/2 tsp. salt

Combine all ingredients. Bake at 350° for 40 to 50 minutes. Bake in tube pan.

Icing for Pumpkin Cake:

1/2 (8 oz.) pkg. cream cheese
1/2 stick butter or margarine
1/2 lb. powdered sugar
1 tsp. vanilla

Combine in order. Beat with mixer for a few minutes. Spread on cool cake.

MAGIC COOKIE BARS — **Bonnie Swecker**

Makes 24 to 36 bars.

1/2 c. margarine or butter
1 1/2 c. graham cracker crumbs
1 (14 oz.) can Eagle Brand sweetened condensed milk (not evaporated milk)
1 (6 oz.) pkg. semi-sweet chocolate chips
1 (3 1/2 oz.) can flaked coconut (1 1/2 c.)
1 c. chopped nuts

Preheat oven to 350° (325° for glass dish). In 13 x 9 baking pan or glass pan melt margarine in oven.

Sprinkle graham cracker crumbs over margarine. Pour sweetened condensed milk evenly over crumbs. Top with remaining ingredients. Press down.

Bake 25 to 30 minutes, or until lightly brown. Cool, chill if desired. Cut into bars. Store loosely covered at room temperature.

TEXAS SHEET CAKE **Portia Morris**
(Amarillo) Assembly of God

In large bowl, sift together:

2 c. sugar
2 c. flour

Mix in large saucepan:

1 stick butter
1/2 c. shortening
4 Tbsp. cocoa
1 c. water

Bring to rapid boil and pour over dry ingredients. Stir well. Add:

1/2 c. buttermilk
1 tsp. vanilla
2 eggs, slightly beaten
1 tsp. soda (baking)

Mix well, pour in greased pan, 16 x 11. Bake 20 minutes at 400°. Topping: 5 minutes before cake is done prepare topping.

Topping:

Melt and bring to boil:

1 stick butter
4 Tbsp. cocoa
6 Tbsp. condensed milk
1 box powdered sugar
1 1/2 c. chopped pecans
1 tsp. vanilla

Mix well and spread on hot cake as soon as it's removed from oven.

VANILLA WAFER BALLS **Bonnie Swecker**

1 (12 oz.) box vanilla wafers, crushed fine
1 c. nuts, chopped fine
1 box powdered sugar
1 (6 oz.) can frozen orange juice, thawed
1 stick margarine, melted

Combine all ingredients. Shape into little balls, and roll in coconut.

"Nice for holidays."

EASY COBBLER

Bonnie Swecker

2 c. self-rising flour
2 c. sugar
1 c. canned milk

Melt 1 stick margarine in pan. Mix above ingredients together and pour in baking dish. Place fruit on top. (You can use any kind of fruit.)

EASY MACAROONS

Bonnie Swecker

2 (8 oz.) pkgs. coconut
1 (15 oz.) can or 1 1/3 c. sweetened condensed milk
2 tsp. vanilla

Mix all ingredients together and drop from teaspoon into well greased cooky sheet. Bake in moderate oven at 350° for 10 to 12 minutes. Cool slightly, remove to rack.

Makes 4 dozen.

CHOCOLATE ECLAIR CAKE

Portia Mae Morris

Butter 9 x 13 pan. Line with whole graham crackers.

2 pkgs. French vanilla instant pudding
3 c. milk

Beat well, add 9-ounce carton Cool Whip. Pour 1/2 mixture over graham crackers, add another layer of graham crackers and remainder of pudding. Top with 3rd layer of graham crackers.

Topping:

2 oz. liquid chocolate
3 Tbsp. soft butter
2 Tbsp. white Karo syrup
3 Tbsp. milk
2 tsp. vanilla
1 1/2 c. powdered sugar

Beat well and pour over grahams.
Refrigerate 24 hours.

CHARLOTTESVILLE CAKE

Ethel Morris
(Pastor Morris' Mother)

1/3 c. milk
3 sticks butter
2 2/3 c. sugar
3 c. (unsifted) flour
6 large eggs
1 tsp. vanilla extract
1 tsp. coconut extract
1 1/4 tsp. baking powder
1 (8 oz.) crushed pineapple
1 c. flaked coconut (+ extra for outside)

1. Thoroughly mix flour and baking powder.
2. In separate bowl, cream butter, sugar, vanilla and coconut (extracts) until fluffy.
3. Beat in eggs, 1 at a time, until thoroughly mixed. Beat into mixture flour and milk (4 portions) until mixed smooth.

Blend in pineapple with juice. Blend in flaked coconut. Bake until done, 1 hour 25 minutes in 325° oven in tube pan.

Cream Cheese Icing:

1 stick butter
1 tsp. vanilla extract
1 lb. 10X sugar

Mix until thick. Spread on cake. Cover with coconut.

PUMPKIN APPLE RING

Bonnie Swecker

1 1/2 c. sugar
1/2 c. butter or margarine
2 eggs
2 medium apples, pared, cored and shredded (1 1/2 c.)
1 c. canned pumpkin
2 c. flour
1 tsp. baking powder
1/2 tsp. baking soda
1/4 tsp. salt
1/2 tsp. ground cinnamon
1/2 tsp. nutmeg
1/4 tsp. ground cloves
1/4 tsp. ground ginger

In a mixing bowl, cream together sugar, butter or margarine, add eggs, one at a time, beating well after each addition. Blend in apples and pumpkin.

Stir together flour, baking powder, soda, salt and spice. Add to pumpkin mixture, stirring until well combined. Put into greased and floured 8-inch fluted tube pan.

Bake in 350° oven for 55 minutes. Cool in pan 10 minutes; remove from pan and cool on wire rack.

Sift powdered sugar over cooled cake.

LEMON DESSERT

Bonnie Swecker

Combine and bake at 350° for 15 minutes:

1 c. flour
1 stick margarine
1/2 c. chopped nuts

Combine and spread over first layer:

1 c. Cool Whip
1 c. powdered sugar
1 (8 oz.) Philadelphia cream cheese
2 small pkgs. instant pudding, lemon or any flavor
3 c. milk

Spread Cool Whip over pudding layer and sprinkle nuts on top.

JELLO AND COTTAGE CHEESE DESSERT

Bonnie Swecker

1 can mandarin oranges, drained
1 small can crushed pineapple, drained
1 box orange jello
1 small container cottage cheese

Mix well, add 8-ounce carton of Cool Whip; mix together.

JELLO DESSERT

Bonnie Swecker

1 1/2 c. graham cracker crumbs
3 Tbsp. sugar
1/4 c. melted margarine
1 (6 oz.) pkg. orange or lime jello
2 c. boiling water
1 (20 oz.) can crushed pineapple, undrained
1 c. diced oranges
1 c. Dream Whip or heavy cream
1 can coconut (optional)

Crust: Combine graham cracker crumbs, sugar and margarine and press into bottom of 13 x 9 x 2 pan. Set aside.

Dissolve jello in boiling water, stir in pineapple and oranges. Chill until slightly thickened.

Mix in 1 cup coconut. Fold in Dream Whip and put in prepared crust. Chill until firm.

SAUERKRAUT SURPRISE CAKE

Julie Burnham

1/2 c. margarine
1 1/2 c. sugar
3 eggs
1 tsp. vanilla
2 c. sifted flour
1 tsp. baking powder
1 tsp. baking soda
1/4 tsp. salt
1/2 c. cocoa
1 c. water
1 (8 oz.) can sauerkraut, drained, rinsed, chopped (I prefer to use 16 oz.)

Cream butter and sugar till light. Beat in eggs, one at a time, add vanilla. Sift together flour, baking powder, soda, salt and cocoa. Add to creamed mixture alternately with water, beating after each addition.

Stir in sauerkraut. Turn into 13 x 9 x 2 pan. Bake at 350° for 35-40 minutes.

Note: I drain the sauerkraut in a colander in the sink. I run water on it. Then I put it in a bowl and I fill the bowl with water and put it in the refrigerator. I do this either overnight or during the day for a few hours. I like to drain it and add fresh water to it a few times before I use it. When I'm ready to use it I drain and rinse it one last time and taste a small piece of sauerkraut. When it is completely TASTELESS it's ready to use. The sauerkraut must be DRAINED and RINSED well.

Sour Cream Chocolate Frosting:

1 (6 oz.) pkg. chocolate pieces
4 Tbsp. butter

Melt over low heat. Remove from heat, blend:

1/2 c. sour cream
1 tsp. vanilla
1/4 tsp. salt

Gradually add 2 1/2-2 3/4 cups confectioners sugar.

DUMP CAKE

Frances Powers

1 can cherry pie filling
1 can crushed pineapple
1 box yellow cake mix
2 sticks melted margarine
1 can coconut
1 c. chopped pecans (optional)

Preheat oven to 350°. Pour into large greased baking dish in order given. Do not mix at all. Bake for 1 hour.

NEW YORK CHEESECAKE — **Laura Fabian**

3 (8 oz.) pkgs. cream cheese
1 pt. sour cream
1 c. sugar plus 3 Tbsp.
3 Tbsp. flour
6 eggs
1 tsp. vanilla

Graham cracker crust for 9-inch springform pan. Follow directions on graham cracker package, grease and line pan with mixture.

1. Beat together softened cream cheese, flour and 1 cup sugar.
2. Separate eggs, adding one yolk at a time, leaving whites in a separate bowl.
3. Beat egg whites with 3 tablespoons sugar until fluffy. Set aside.
4. Add sour cream and vanilla to cream cheese mixture.
5. Fold in egg whites until smooth.
6. Pour mixture into springform pan.
7. Bake at 325° for 1 hour. Place a pan of hot water on the lower rack of the oven.

JEWISH APPLE CAKE — **Ruth Baber**

3 c. flour
2 1/2 c. sugar
1 c. oil
4 eggs
1/2 tsp. salt
2 tsp. baking powder
1/2 c. orange juice
2 1/2 tsp. vanilla
4 large apples
2 tsp. cinnamon
5 Tbsp. sugar

Peel, core and slice apples. Add 2 teaspoons cinnamon and 5 tablespoons sugar. Mix and set aside.

In separate bowl, mix remaining ingredients - flour, sugar, oil, eggs, salt, baking powder, orange juice, vanilla and mix well. Batter will be very thick.

Layer batter and apples in greased and floured tube pan, beginning and ending with batter.

Bake at 350° for 1 hour 45 minutes. Cool in pan 1 hour before removing cake.

RICE PUDDING WITH RASPBERRY SAUCE Kathy Letson

2/3 c. sugar
1/2 c. water
2 envelopes unflavored gelatin
1/2 tsp. salt
2 c. milk
1 1/2 c. cooked rice
2 tsp. vanilla
1 c. whipping cream
Raspberry Sauce (recipe follows)

Heat sugar, water, gelatin and salt in 2-quart saucepan, stirring constantly, until gelatin is dissolved, about 1 minute. Stir in milk, rice and vanilla. Place saucepan in bowl of iced water, stirring occasionally, until mixture mounds slightly when dropped from a spoon, about 10 minutes.

Beat whipping cream in chilled bowl until stiff. Fold whipped cream into rice mixture. Pour into ungreased 6-cup mold or serving bowl. Cover and refrigerate until firm, about 3 hours. Unmold by dipping briefly in warm water and loosening edge with spatula; invert on serving plate. Serve with Raspberry Sauce.

Raspberry Sauce:

1 (10 oz.) pkg. frozen raspberries, thawed
1 Tbsp. cold water
2 tsp. cornstarch

Heat raspberries (with syrup) to boiling. Mix water and cornstarch; stir into raspberries. Heat to boiling, stirring constantly. Boil and stir 1 minute. Cool, press through sieve to remove seeds.

BLACK BOTTOM CUPCAKES Ruth Baber

Mixture #1:

8 oz. cream cheese, softened
1 egg
1/3 c. sugar
1/8 tsp. salt
6 oz. (1 c.) chocolate chips

Mixture #2:

1 1/2 c. flour
1 c. sugar
1/4 c. cocoa
1 tsp. baking soda
1 tsp. vanilla
1/2 tsp. salt
1 c. water
1/3 c. oil
1 Tbsp. vinegar

Mixture #1: Beat egg slightly in small bowl. Add cream

cheese, 1/3 cup sugar, 1/8 teaspoon salt and beat until smooth. Add in 6 ounces chocolate chips and mix with fork. Set aside.

Mixture #2: Add all ingredients - 1 1/2 cups flour, 1 cup sugar, 1/4 cup cocoa, 1 teaspoon baking soda, 1/2 teaspoon salt, 1 cup water, 1/3 cup oil, 1 teaspoon vanilla and 1 tablespoon vinegar. Combine and beat well.

Fill up cupcake papers 1/3 full with mixture #2. Drop teaspoon of mixture #1 on top.

Bake at 350° for 20-25 minutes.

OREO ICE CREAM CAKE

Ruth Baber

- 1 1/4 lbs. Oreo cookies, crushed in blender (set aside 1 c.)
- 1/2 gal. vanilla ice cream, softened
- 1 Tbsp. margarine
- 8 oz. Hershey syrup
- large Cool Whip, thawed

Take 1 tablespoon margarine and blend with cookies. Spread on bottom of 13 x 9 x 2 pan for crust. Spread softened ice cream on top of cookie crust. Cover with chocolate syrup. Cover syrup with Cool Whip and sprinkle on 1 cup of reserved crushed cookies. Sprinkle with chocolate chips, if desired. Keep in freezer.

AUNT LOUISE'S POUND CAKE

Kris Leonard

- 3/4 lb. butter
- 1 lb. box confectioners sugar
- 6 eggs
- 1 lb. box cake flour
- 1/3 c. milk
- 1/2 tsp. each: vanilla, lemon and almond extracts

Mix together and bake at 350° for 1-2 hours.

BREAD PUDDING SAUCE

Madeline Nelson
(Kris Miller's Mom)

- 1 c. sugar
- 3 Tbsp. cornstarch
- 2 c. water
- 1 stick margarine
- 1 tsp. vanilla extract

Mix sugar, cornstarch and water. Cook until it thickens and turns clear. Around the boiling point. Add oleo and vanilla. Serve warm over pudding.

AUNT FRANCES' ALMOND PRALINE CAKE Kris Leonard

Bake 2 (9-inch) layers yellow or white cake.

Frosting:

1 (6 oz.) pkg. butterscotch pieces	1/4 tsp. salt
1 c. brown sugar	2 Tbsp. butter
1/2 c. whipping cream	1 c. slivered almonds
2 Tbsp. light corn syrup	1 tsp. vanilla

Combine butterscotch pieces, brown sugar, cream, corn syrup, salt in saucepan and bring to a boil, stirring until pieces melt, boil gently, stirring constantly, add butter and cool 10 minutes. Add nuts and vanilla, beat briefly with wooden spoon until it's of spreading consistency. Frost cake.

COFFEE ANGEL FOOD CAKE Libby Gray

Cake:

1 box angel food cake mix	1 Tbsp. instant coffee

Dissolve coffee in water before mixing with cake-following box directions. Bake according to instructions.

Icing:

3/4 c. unsalted butter	4-6 Tbsp. milk
1/4 tsp. salt	1 1/2 tsp. vanilla
3 3/4 c. sifted confectioners sugar	2-3 Tbsp. instant coffee
	toasted almond slivers

Cream butter, add salt and sugar, small amounts at a time. Dissolve coffee in milk, add milk and vanilla to sugar mixture as needed. Beat until light and fluffy.

Ice cake and top with almonds.

BLACK WALNUT CAKE

Misty Frye

1 c. butter
1 lb. powdered sugar
5 eggs, beaten
1 tsp. vanilla
1 c. chopped black walnuts
3 c. flour (self-rising)
1/2 tsp. salt
1 c. milk

Preheat oven to 350°.

Cream butter and sugar until smooth. Add eggs and vanilla. Beat with mixer until well mixed. Add walnuts; mix well.

Sift flour and salt. Stir into creamed mixture alternately with milk, starting and ending with flour. Pour into a greased and floured tube pan. Bake for 1 hour.

CHOCOLATE HAYSTACKS

Misty Frye

1/3 c. plus 1 Tbsp. shredded coconut
1 (3 oz.) can chow mein noodles
1 c. semi-sweet chocolate chips, melted and cooled

Mix 1/3 cup coconut and the noodles in a medium-size bowl. Add melted chocolate. Mix well. Drop 12 mounds of noodle mixture onto waxed-paper lined cookie sheet. Press mounds to compact. Sprinkle with remaining coconut. Chill until firm. Makes 12 cookies.

NO-BAKE PEANUT BUTTER COOKIES

Paula Scheerer

1 1/2 c. sugar
1/2 c. butter
3/4 c. flour
1/2 c. milk
1 1/2 c. quick oats
2/3 c. peanut butter
1/2 c. chopped nuts
1/2 c. coconut
1 tsp. vanilla
1/4 tsp. salt

Combine in saucepan: sugar, butter, flour and milk. Bring to a full boil and boil hard for 3 minutes, stirring constantly. Remove from heat and add remaining ingredients. Blend well.

Drop by spoonfuls onto foil or greased cookie sheet. Cool.

PUMPKIN ROLL CAKE

Ruth Baber

Mixture #1:

3 eggs
1 c. sugar
2/3 c. canned pumpkin
1 tsp. lemon juice
3/4 c. flour
1 tsp. baking powder
2 tsp. cinnamon
1 tsp. ginger
1/2 tsp. nutmeg
1/2 tsp. salt
1 c. finely chopped walnuts

Mixture #2:

1 c. powdered sugar
2 (3 oz.) pkgs. cream cheese, softened
4 Tbsp. margarine
1/2 tsp. vanilla

Beat 3 eggs on high speed for 5 minutes; gradually beat in 1 cup sugar. Stir in 2/3 cup pumpkin and 1 teaspoon lemon juice.

In separate bowl, combine 3/4 cup flour, 1 teaspoon baking powder, 2 teaspoons cinnamon, 1 teaspoon ginger, 1/2 teaspoon nutmeg and 1/2 teaspoon salt. Fold into pumpkin mixture.

Spread into greased and floured 15 x 10 x 1-inch pan. Top with 1 cup finely chopped walnuts. Bake at 375° for 15 minutes. While still hot, turn out onto dish towel, sprinkle with powdered sugar, starting at narrow end, roll towel and cake together. Cool in refrigerator for 1 hour.

Unroll and fill with mixture #2.

Mixture #2 - Filling: Beat ingredients until smooth, spread over cake, roll and chill.

TEXAS SHEET CAKE

Ruth Baber

1. Bring to boil:

2 sticks margarine
1 c. water
4 heaping Tbsp. cocoa

2. Remove from heat. Add to saucepan:

2 c. sugar
2 c. flour
1/2 tsp. salt

3. Beat in:

2 eggs
1/2 c. sour cream
1 tsp. baking soda

4. Pour in greased and floured 15 x 10 x 1 pan. Bake for 25 minutes at 325°.

5. Five minutes before cake is due to be removed from oven, using same pan, bring to boil:

1 stick margarine
4 Tbsp. cocoa
6 Tbsp. milk

6. Remove from heat, add and beat in with mixer:

1 tsp. vanilla
1 box confectionary sugar

7. Spread over cake as soon as you take it from oven.

8. Refrigerate until cooled.

Note: If icing is too thick and not pourable, add more milk.

CHEESE CAKE

Ruth Baber

Preheat oven 15 minutes.

Crust:

1 1/2 c. graham cracker crumbs
3 Tbsp. brown sugar
1 tsp. cinnamon
6 Tbsp. melted margarine

Mix together well with hands. Press in bottom of buttered springform pan.

Filling:

3 (8 oz.) pkgs. cream cheese
1 1/2 c. sugar
4 medium eggs
1 (16 oz.) sour cream
2 Tbsp. lemon juice
1/2 tsp. vanilla
1/2 pt. whipping cream

Cream cheese with mixer, add sugar until fluffy. Add eggs, one at a time, while beating. Add sour cream, whipping cream, vanilla and lemon juice. Beat until fluffy.

Bake 1 hour at 350°. Turn off oven and leave cake in oven 1 hour. Sit out for 1 hour. Refrigerate for 8 hours.

ELLA BAGGETT'S POUND CAKE — Jim Fruengel

3 sticks butter (not margarine), softened
3 c. sugar
10 eggs
3 c. sifted cake flour
1 tsp. vanilla
1 Tbsp. butternut flavoring

Cream butter, gradually add sugar, beat until light and fluffy. Add eggs, one at a time, beating well after each addition. Gradually add flour, 1/2 cup at a time. Stir in flavorings by hand.

Pour batter into a greased and floured 10-inch tube pan or 3 loaf pans. Put into a cold oven and then turn oven to 300° and bake for 1 1/2 hours. DO NOT OPEN OVEN DOOR WHILE BAKING. Cool in pan for 15 minutes. And then cool on wire rack.

Let butter and eggs sit out overnight.

BLACK WALNUT POUND CAKE — Jim Fruengel

2 sticks margarine, softened
3 c. sugar
1/4 tsp. salt
1/2 c. Crisco shortening
5 eggs
3 c. flour
3/4 c. Pet milk (add enough water to make 1 c.)
2 c. chopped black walnuts (dredged in 4 Tbsp. of the 3 c. flour)
2 Tbsp. maple flavoring

Cream together the first 4 ingredients. Add eggs, one at a time. Add flour with milk beginning and ending with flour. Fold in nuts and flavoring.

Pour batter into a 10-inch tube pan (that's been greased and floured). Start in a cold oven and then turn oven on to 325° and bake for 1 hour 35 minutes.

DO NOT OPEN OVEN DOOR WHILE BAKING.

BROWN SUGAR POUND CAKE — Jim Fruengel

1 box light brown sugar
3 sticks butter (not margarine)
7 eggs
3 c. cake flour

Cream butter and sugar until light and fluffy. Add eggs, one at a time. Fold in flour. Pour into a greased and floured tube pan that has been lined with wax paper on the bottom.

Bake at 325° for 1 1/2 hours. Cool in pan for 15 minutes. Peel off paper.

RAISIN OATMEAL COOKIES

Paula Scheerer

1/2 c. shortening
1 c. sugar
2 eggs
1/4 c. milk
1 1/2 c. flour
1 tsp. baking soda
1 tsp. baking powder
1/2 tsp. salt
1 2/3 c. rolled oats
1 c. seedless raisins
1 tsp. cinnamon

Rinse raisins in hot water and drain. Mix shortening with sugar. Add beaten eggs and milk. Combine with oatmeal, raisins and mix well. Mix flour, soda, baking powder, salt, cinnamon together, then combine with other mixture. Beat thoroughly.

Drop onto greased pan and bake about 12 minutes at 350°-375°. Makes about 3 dozen medium-sized cookies.

CHOCOLATE-PECAN POUND CAKE

Jim Fruengel

3 sticks butter (not margarine)
2 1/2 c. sugar
6 eggs
3 c. cake flour
1 1/2 tsp. baking powder
1 c. milk
12 oz. chocolate chips, melted
2 c. chopped pecans

Cream butter, gradually add sugar and beat till light and fluffy. Add eggs, one at a time, beating well after each addition.

Add flour and baking powder, alternating with milk, beginning and ending with flour and baking powder. Add the melted chocolate chips and blend well. Stir in chopped pecans.

Pour batter in a greased and floured tube pan. That's been lined with wax paper (on the bottom). Bake at 325° for 1 hour and 15 minutes. Cool in pan for 15 minutes. Cool completely on wire rack.

"NO BAKE" COOKIES

Ruth Hale

2 c. sugar
4 Tbsp. cocoa
1/4 c. margarine
1/2 c. milk
dash salt
2 c. quick oats
1/2 c. peanut butter
1 tsp. vanilla

Combine sugar, margarine, milk and salt. Bring to a boil in saucepan. Boil 1 minute, stirring occasionally. Add oats, peanut butter and vanilla. Drop by teaspoon onto waxed paper. Cool.

CARROT CAKE

Frances Powers

4 eggs
2 c. sugar
3 c. shredded carrots
1 1/2 c. Wesson oil
1 c. black walnuts
2 or 3 tsp. walnut flavoring
2 c. self-rising flour
1 Tbsp. cinnamon

Mix all ingredients together in large bowl. Bake for 1 hour, 15 minutes at 350°. Let cake cool and pour on glaze.

Glaze:

1/2 c. sugar
1/4 c. buttermilk
1/4 tsp. vanilla
1/4 tsp. baking soda
1 1/2 tsp. Karo syrup

Mix and boil 2 or 3 minutes.

RED CHRISTMAS CAKE - GATEAU ROUGE DE NOEL

Frances Powers

1/2 c. shortening
1 1/2 c. sugar
2 oz. red food coloring
2 c. cake flour
1 Tbsp. cocoa
1 tsp. salt
2 eggs
1 c. buttermilk
1 Tbsp. vinegar
3 tsp. vanilla
1 tsp. baking soda

Cream sugar and shortening until light and fluffy. Add food coloring and eggs, one at a time, beating well after each addition. Sift the flour 3 times with cocoa and salt into another bowl. Add these dry ingredients alternately with the buttermilk to the sugar mixture. Mix well. Add vanilla and beat well, at least 2 minutes, at high speed (using electric mixer). Dissolve soda in vinegar and fold into batter - do not beat.

Pour into 2 (9-inch) cake pans which have been greased and floured and bake at 350° for 35 minutes.

White Snow Cap Frosting:

1 1/2 c. sugar (bar sugar or extra fine)
1 stick margarine
1/2 c. shortening
5 3/4 Tbsp. flour
1 c. milk
1 tsp. vanilla
pinch salt

Mix together the flour, salt and milk in saucepan and cook until the consistency of a thick pudding - stirring constantly. Set aside to cool.

Cream margarine and shortening together. Add sugar and vanilla. Add flour mixture to sugar mixture and spread over cake.

"Decorate for the occasion. This is a beautiful, delicious cake - once seen and eaten, it is never forgotten!"

CHRISTMAS APPLESAUCE CAKE

Ruth Hale

1 can (2 c.) applesauce
2 1/2 c. flour
1 1/2 tsp. baking soda
1 tsp. salt
1/2 tsp. cinnamon
1/2 tsp. nutmeg
2 Tbsp. cocoa
1 1/2 c. sugar
1/2 c. shortening
1/2 box raisins (1 c.)
1 c. walnuts
1 small bottle cherries (with juice), (1 c.)

Cream together sugar and shortening. Sift together dry ingredients and add alternately with applesauce. Add raisins, nuts and cherries and mix thoroughly.

Bake in tube pan about 1 hour or more in 350° oven.

RED VELVET CAKE

Ruth Hale

1 c. shortening
2 1/4 c. flour
1 1/2 c. sugar
2 eggs
1 tsp. soda
1/2 tsp. salt
1 tsp. vanilla
1 c. buttermilk
2 Tbsp. cocoa
1/4 c. red food coloring
1 Tbsp. vinegar

Cream sugar and shortening together. Add eggs, salt and food coloring. Mix vanilla with buttermilk and add alternately with flour and cocoa. Put soda into vinegar and blend. Add to batter.

Bake at 350° for 30 minutes in 8-inch round pan; 40 minutes for 9 x 13-inch pan.

Icing:

1 c. milk
3 Tbsp. flour

Blend and cook until thick. Cool. Cream:

2 sticks butter
1 c. sugar

Add 1 teaspoon vanilla. Whip all together until fluffy (about 3 minutes).

APPLE WALNUT RING CAKE

Doris Sharp

1 c. butter or margarine
2 c. sugar
3 eggs
3 c. sifted all-purpose flour
1 1/2 tsp. baking soda
1/2 tsp. salt
1 tsp. cinnamon
1/4 tsp. mace
2 tsp. vanilla
3 c. chopped apples
2 c. chopped walnuts

Cream butter and sugar until fluffy. Add eggs, one at a time, beating well after each addition. Mix and sift flour, baking soda, salt, cinnamon and mace and add gradually.

Stir in vanilla, apples and walnuts. Batter will be stiff. Spoon into greased and floured 10-inch tube pan.

Bake at 325° for 1 1/2 hours. Let cool in pan for 10 minutes. Remove to rack.

14 CARAT NO SUGAR CAKE

Barbara Shenahan

2 c. flour
1 1/2 tsp. baking soda
2 tsp. cinnamon
1 1/2 c. oil
2 c. grated raw carrots
1/2 c. chopped nuts
2 tsp. baking powder
1 tsp. salt
30 pkgs. Equal
4 eggs
1 (8 oz.) can crushed pineapple, drained

Sift together flour, baking powder, baking soda, salt, cinnamon.

Add sugar, oil and eggs. Mix well. Stir in carrots, pineapple and nuts.

Bake in 13 x 9 x 2 pan for 35-40 minutes at 350°. Cool in pan and then on wire racks.

Frosting:

1 stick butter
1 tsp. vanilla
8 oz. cream cheese
1 lb. box powdered sugar, sifted

Mix together and frost.

AGRESSION COOKIES

Julie Burnham

3 c. rolled oats
1 1/2 c. brown sugar
1 1/2 c. flour
1 1/2 c. margarine, softened
1 1/2 tsp. baking powder

Place all ingredients in a large bowl. Mash them, knead them, pound them with your hands. The longer and harder you mix, the better the cookies.

Form into small balls and place on greased cookie sheets. Bake 10-12 minutes. Makes about 5-6 dozen. Add raisins, nuts, etc.

PUMPKIN CHEESECAKE BARS

Portia Mae Morris

1 c. all-purpose flour
1/3 c. packed brown sugar
5 Tbsp. butter
1 c. finely chopped pecans
8 oz. softened cream cheese
3/4 c. sugar
1/2 c. solid-pack pumpkin
2 eggs, slightly beaten
1 1/2 tsp. ground cinnamon
1 tsp. ground allspice
1 tsp. vanilla extract

Combine flour and brown sugar in medium bowl, cut in butter to make a crumb mixture. Stir in nuts. (Set aside 3/4 cup mixture for topping.) Press remaining mixture into bottom of 8 x 8 x 1 1/2-inch baking dish.

Bake in preheated 350° oven for 15 minutes. Cool slightly.

Combine cream cheese, sugar, pumpkin, eggs, cinnamon, allspice and vanilla in large mixer bowl. Blend until smooth. Pour over baked crust. Sprinkle with reserved topping. Bake an additional 30-35 minutes. Cool before cutting into bars.

Makes 32 (1 x 2-inch) bar cookies.

BLENDER CHEESE CAKE

Barbara Shenahan

1 c. sugar
1 c. milk
4 eggs
2 Tbsp. cornstarch
1 tsp. vanilla
2 (8 oz.) pkgs. cream cheese

Blend all above ingredients together in blender. Grease 10-inch pie plate with margarine. Pour in above mixture.

Bake 1 hour 10 minutes at 325°.

LEMON DELIGHT

Portia Mae Morris

1 c. confectioners sugar
2 c. flour
2 sticks butter
3 c. chopped walnuts
3 small boxes lemon pudding
1 1/2 lbs. Philadelphia cream cheese
largest size Cool Whip
4 1/2 c. milk

Mix together flour, butter and 1 1/2 cups walnuts. Spread in baking dish (9 x 13) and pat till solid. Much like pie dough. Bake at 350° for 30 minutes. Let cool.

Blend cream cheese, sugar, 2 cups Cool Whip and 1 cup nuts. Spread on top.

Blend pudding and milk, fold in 1 cup Cool Whip. Cover with remaining Cool Whip and nuts.

CHOCOLATE COOL

Portia Mae Morris

1 c. confectioners sugar
2 c. flour
2 sticks butter
3 c. chopped walnuts
3 small boxes chocolate pudding
1 1/2 lbs. cream cheese
largest size Cool Whip
4 1/2 c. milk
1/2 c. chocolate chips, finely chopped

Mix together flour, butter and 1 1/2 cups nuts. Pat firmly in 9 x 13 baking dish. Bake at 350° for 30 minutes. Let cool completely! (Place chocolate chips in blender to chop till chocolate powder forms.)

Blend cream cheese, sugar, 2 cups Cool Whip, 1 cup nuts. Spread on top of crust.

Blend pudding, milk and 2/3 (powdered) chocolate chips. Spread on top of cheese mix.

Cover with remaining Cool Whip. Sprinkle remaining chocolate powder and nuts.

LUSCIOUS LEMON LAYER CAKE

Portia Mae Morris

1/2 c. shortening
1 3/4 c. sugar
6 egg yolks
2 1/2 c. sifted cake flour
2 1/2 tsp. baking powder
1/2 tsp. salt
1 c. plus 3 Tbsp. milk
1 Tbsp. grated lemon rind

Cream shortening; add sugar, beating at medium speed of an electric mixer. Combine flour, baking powder and salt; add to creamed mixture alternately with milk, beginning and ending with flour mixture. Stir in lemon rind.

Pour batter into 2 greased and floured 9-inch round cake pans. Bake at 350° for 25-30 minutes or till wooden pick inserted in center comes out clean. Cool in pans 10 minutes; remove and let cool completely. Spread Lemon Buttercream Frosting on sides and layers.

Lemon Buttercream Frosting:

1/2 c. butter, softened
1 egg yolk
16 oz. 10X sugar (powdered), sifted
1 tsp. grated lemon rind
6 Tbsp. lemon juice

Cream butter, add egg yolk and beat well. Add powdered sugar, beating well. Add remaining ingredients, beating until smooth.

SPICED PECANS

Portia Mae Morris

1 lb. shelled pecans
1 c. sugar
1 egg white, slightly beaten
1 Tbsp. water
1 tsp. cinnamon
1/4 tsp. salt

Preheat oven to 200°. Mix sugar, egg white, water, cinnamon and salt. Add nuts. Mix thoroughly. Spread on baking pan.

Bake for 45 minutes, turning frequently until nuts turn white. Serve in doily lined basket - these make nice holiday hostess gifts.

BLUEBERRY SALAD

Shirley Sadler
Pastor Morris' Cousin

large box either grape or blackberry jello
1 (No. 10) can crushed pineapple
1 can blueberry pie filling
1 c. hot water

Mix all ingredients together and let jel in 9 x 13 x 2-inch dish.

8 oz. sour cream
8 oz. cream cheese
1 c. chopped walnuts
1 c. 10X powdered sugar

Mix together and place on top of jelled fruit.

BRIDE'S SALAD

Ethel Morris
Pastor's Mom

May be used as dessert.

1 box lemon jello
1/2 c. sugar
1 c. hot water
1 c. cottage cheese
1 c. crushed pineapple
1 c. chopped pecans
1 large Cool Whip
4 doz. mini marshmallows
1 c. cocoanut
maraschino cherries, sliced in half

Mix first 3 ingredients. Let cool. Add rest of ingredients. Sprinkle cocoanut on top. Garnish with cherries and pecans.

MAMA'S FAVORITE CAKE

Ethel Morris
(Pastor's Mother)

Cake:

1 box Duncan Hines yellow cake mix
4 eggs
1/2 c. milk
1 can mandarin oranges with juice

Topping:

1 (9-inch) Cool Whip
1 large can crushed pineapple with juice
1 box vanilla instant pudding

(Use 3 (8-inch) cake pans.)

Mix first 4 ingredients and bake at 350° till done (test with toothpick). Let cool.

Mix topping ingredients and keep refrigerated.

HOT FUDGE SAUCE

Portia Mae Morris

4 oz. unsweetened chocolate
3 Tbsp. butter
2/3 c. boiling water
1 1/2 c. sugar
6 Tbsp. corn syrup
1 Tbsp. rum extract

Melt chocolate and butter slowly in heavy pan. Add boiling water and stir well. Add sugar and corn syrup and mix till smooth. Turn up heat. Stir until mixture boils.

Adjust heat so it is just slightly boiling. Cook, but do not stir, for 10 minutes. Remove from heat - add rum extract.

CHOCOLATE TORTE

Phil Wagener

1 c. all-purpose flour
1/2 c. butter
3/4 c. ground walnuts
1 Tbsp. water
8 oz. cream cheese
1 c. 10X sugar
2 large bowls Cool Whip
2 boxes chocolate pudding

1. Combine flour, 1/2 cup walnuts, butter and water. Mix and spread on 9 x 13-inch pan. Bake 12 minutes at 350°.
2. Combine cream cheese, sugar with fork, then add 1 bowl Cool Whip, then spread on as 2nd layer of pan.
3. Prepare chocolate pudding. Let cool 1/2 hour and put on as 3rd layer.
4. Use 1 large bowl of Cool Whip as 4th layer (top).
5. Sprinkle nuts on top. Let cool in refrigerator for 1 1/2 hours.

GINGER COOKIES

Julie Burnham

3/4 c. Crisco
1 c. sugar
1 beaten egg
1/4 c. molasses
2 c. flour
1 Tbsp. ginger
2 tsp. baking soda
1 tsp. cinnamon
1/2 tsp. salt

Cream together Crisco and sugar, add egg and molasses. Stir together the remaining ingredients and add to creamed mixture. Form into small balls. Roll in sugar.

Place on ungreased cookie sheet. Bake at 350° for 10-15 minutes.

BUTTERNUT POUND CAKE

Linda Murphy

3 c. sugar
1/2 c. Crisco
3 c. flour
1 c. milk
2 sticks margarine
5 eggs
1/2 tsp. salt
2 Tbsp. butternut flavor

Mix sugar, Crisco, margarine, salt. Add eggs, one at a time. Add flour and milk alternately. Fold in flavoring by hand.

*Start in cold oven. Bake 1 hour 45 minutes at 325°. Bake in greased tube pan.

CARAMEL GLAZE

Mary Parsons

1/3 c. evaporated milk
2 Tbsp. brown sugar
1 1/2 c. powdered sugar
1 tsp. vanilla

Combine evaporated milk and brown sugar in saucepan over medium heat, cook, stirring constantly, until mixture begins to boil.

Place milk mixture, powdered sugar and vanilla in bowl. Mix on medium to high speed until creamy, about 3 minutes.

POOR MAN'S RICH CAKE

Lois Middleton

1 lb. raisins
1/2 c. shortening
1 c. sugar
1 c. brown sugar
1 tsp. cloves
1 tsp. nutmeg
1 tsp. cinnamon
1 tsp. salt
1 Tbsp. baking soda
4 c. flour
1 c. nuts
1 jar maraschino cherries (small)

Stew raisins in 2 cups water for 15 minutes. Remove from heat, add 1 cup cold water.

In large mixing bowl, add all ingredients in order. Then stir in raisins. Mix for about 3 minutes. Pour batter in a greased 10-inch tube pan.

Bake at 325° for 1 hour 20 minutes. Garnish top with some nuts and cherries.

This is a good holiday cake if you don't like all the fruity stuff.

GRANDMA'S SPICE CAKE

Sherry Heward

2 c. sugar
1 1/3 c. vegetable shortening
4 eggs
1 1/3 c. sour milk
2 tsp. baking soda
3 to 3 1/2 c. all-purpose flour
1 c. chopped walnuts
1 c. raisins
2 tsp. each: ground allspice, nutmeg and cinnamon
4 drops vanilla extract

1. In a large mixing bowl, beat together sugar and shortening. Add eggs, one at a time, beating well after each addition.

2. In separate bowl, combine the sour milk and baking soda. Stir into first mixture.

3. Stir 3 tablespoons of the flour into the walnuts and raisins, coating well. Add remaining flour and spices to sugar mixture, beating until well combined.

4. With a spoon, stir in vanilla, walnuts and raisins, mixing well. Pour mixture into 3 greased and floured 9-inch round cake pans.

5. Bake at 350° for 55 minutes or until cake tests done. Cool on racks for 10 minutes.

HERSHEY'S DARK CHOCOLATE CAKE — Debbie Caldwell

1 3/4 c. unsifted flour
2 c. sugar
3/4 c. Hershey's cocoa
1 1/2 tsp. baking soda
1 1/2 tsp. baking powder
1 tsp. salt
2 eggs
1 c. milk
1/2 c. vegetable oil
2 tsp. vanilla
1 c. boiling water

1. Combine dry ingredients in large mixing bowl.
2. Add remaining ingredients except boiling water; beat at medium speed for 2 minutes.
3. Remove from mixer; stir in boiling water (batter will be thin).
4. Pour into 2 greased and floured layer or tube pan(s).
5. Bake at 350° for 30 to 35 minutes. Cool 10 minutes. Remove from pan(s) and top with favorite icing.

OLD FASHIONED BUTTER CAKE — Sherry Heward

1 c. butter
2 c. sugar
1 tsp. vanilla extract
4 eggs
3 c. all-purpose flour
1 tsp. baking soda
1 tsp. salt
1 c. buttermilk

1. Beat together butter and sugar until fluffy.
2. Beat in vanilla. Add eggs, one at a time, blending well after each addition.
3. Combine flour with baking soda and salt. Add to batter alternately with buttermilk, beginning and ending with flour.
4. Butter and flour an 8-cup fluted mold. Pour in batter.
5. Bake at 350° for about 1 1/2 hours or until a tester inserted in center comes out clean. Allow cake to stand 5 minutes. Invert.

Remove cake from pan and finish cooling on a rack. Dust with powdered sugar.

BANANA PUDDING (COUNTRY-STYLE)

Mable Lawson
Sherlie Hale

1 box vanilla wafers
1 bunch bananas (ripe), (6 bananas)
2 small boxes vanilla pudding (instant)
1 lb. sour cream
1 large container whip cream
4 c. milk

Combine pudding mix and milk, mix on medium speed for 2 to 3 minutes. Fold in sour cream and whipped cream to pudding.

In large container spread a layer of wafers, then cover with a layer of bananas and a layer of pudding. Repeat this process until all wafers and bananas are used, ending with the pudding on top. Last you take your crumbs from wafers and sprinkle on top of pudding.

CHOCOLATE FILLED BON BONS

Bobbi Dorsey

(My favorite Christmas cookie.)

3/4 c. shortening
1/2 c. sugar
1/4 c. brown sugar
1 egg
2 tsp. vanilla
1/2 tsp. almond extract
1 3/4 c. flour
1/2 tsp. baking powder
1/2 tsp. salt
1/2 c. very finely chopped almonds or pecans
3 1/2 to 4 doz. Hershey Kisses

Preheat oven to 350°. Using mixer, cream shortening and sugars till fluffy. Add egg and extracts, beat well. Add flour, baking powder, salt and nuts. Mix till blended.

Form into 1-inch balls. Press each ball around a Hershey Kiss so it is completely enclosed. Bake 12 minutes on ungreased cookie sheet. Cool on wire racks.

RICOTTA CAKE

Becky Marcucci

1 yellow cake mix with pudding
3 eggs
1/2 c. sugar
2 tsp. vanilla
1 1/2 lbs. Ricotta cheese

Mix cake according to package directions. Place in greased 9 x 13 baking dish.

Mix Ricotta, eggs, sugar and vanilla. Spoon over cake mix.

Bake at 350° for approximately 1 hour or until toothpick inserted in center of cake is clean.

ENGLISH TRIFLE

Kathrenai P. Letson

1 large sponge cake (light)
2 bananas
2 large boxes jello
2 lbs. strawberries, frozen or fresh
2 cans mixed fruit
2 pkgs. vanilla pudding

Make cake or buy light sponge cake. Cut cake in four slices. Put in one slice in bowl.

Note: Make jello with only 1 1/2 cups of hot water and 1 1/2 cups of cold water. Let cool.

Make pudding as package says, let cool.

Top slice with cut-up strawberries, about 1/4 to a 1/2 cup. Put mixed fruit on top of that. Put another slice of cake over that. Cut up bananas. Mix with strawberries and mixed fruit. Do this till you reach almost top.

Pour pudding into jello and mix. Pour all over cake and fruit. Put in refrigerator overnight. Top with whip cream before serving.

ORANGE COCONUT CAKE

Mary Parsons

1 (3 oz.) pkg. orange flavor gelatin
1 1/3 c. flaked coconut
1 box white cake mix (2-layer size)
1 pkg. white frosting (mix or ready-to-spread)

Preheat oven to 375°F.

Measure 1 tablespoon of gelatin into a jar. Add coconut; cover and shake until coconut is evenly tinted.

Prepare cake mix as directed on package, adding remaining gelatin before baking. Bake in 2 (9-inch) layer pans which have been greased and floured and then lined on bottoms with waxed paper. Cool in pans 10 minutes.

Remove from pans and finish cooling on racks. Prepare frosting (if using mix) as directed on package. Frost between layers, assemble cake. Frost top and sides of cake and cover with tinted coconut.

PEANUT BUTTER TANDY CAKE — Debbie Caldwell

1 c. milk
4 beaten eggs
1 tsp. vanilla
pinch salt
2 Tbsp. butter
2 c. flour
2 c. sugar
1 tsp. baking powder

Scald milk and butter. In large bowl, mix eggs, vanilla, salt, flour, sugar and baking powder. Add milk mixture.

Pour into greased and floured jelly roll pan. Bake 25 minutes at 350°. Cool for 5 minutes.

Spread top of cake with peanut butter (just enough to cover cake). Refrigerate for 15 minutes.

Melt 8-ounce Hershey bar in double boiler (or microwave), spread over peanut butter.

Chill and cut into squares.

*If you don't go by the correct (min.) it won't turn out right.

"GOOD GOOGA-MOOGA" — Bonnie Carter

1 (6 oz.) pkg. Jell-O gelatin, any flavor!
1 small container Cool Whip
1 small can crushed pineapple, drained
1 small container cottage cheese

Dump all ingredients into a medium-size bowl and stir till well blended. Chill 1 hour before serving.

(You can really cut the calories on this by using sugar-free gelatin and low-fat cottage cheese.)

DUNDEE CAKE — Kathy Kitchen (Letson)

This most traditional of English cakes is filled with candied fruits and nutmeats, and flavored with citrus rinds. It bakes into a handsome 8-inch round cake. Serve this moist, rich cake in thin wedges, accompanied by piping hot tea.

3/4 c. unsalted butter
3/4 c. sugar
4 whole eggs
2 c. all-purpose flour
1 1/4 tsp. baking powder
1/2 tsp. salt
1/4 c. ground almonds
1 c. currants
1 c. seedless raisins
1/2 c. mixed candied fruit peel, chopped
1/4 c. candied cherries, split
grated rind of 1 large orange
grated rind of 1 lemon
1/3 c. whole blanched almonds

Cream together butter and sugar until thick, fluffy and

ZUCCHINI BREAD OR MUFFINS

Servings : 4

1 cup oil
2 cups sugar
3 eggs
3 teaspoons vanilla
3 cups grated zucchini
3 cups flour
1 teaspoon salt

Beat oil and sugar, then add 1 teaspoon baking soda and 1 teaspoon baking powder, 3 teaspoons cinnamon and 1 cup walnuts. Bake at 350 degrees for 55-60 minutes.

ZUCCHINI BREAD

Servings : 4

- 3 eggs
- 1 cup vegetable oil
- 2 cups sugar
- 2 cups grated zucchini
- 2 teaspoons vanilla
- Chopped nuts (optional)
- 3 cups flour
- 1 teaspoon baking soda
- 1 teaspoon salt
- 3 teaspoons cinnamon
- 1/2 teaspoon baking powder

Preheat oven at 325 degrees. Beat eggs until light. Add oil, sugar, zucchini and nuts, if desired. Combine flour, baking soda, salt, cinnamon, and baking powder. Add egg mixture and mix until well blended. Pour batter in loaf pans.

Bake at 325 degrees for 1 hour. Makes 3 loaves.

light in color. Add eggs, one at a time and continue beating.

Sift together the flour, salt and baking powder. Add to egg mixture, beating in a bit at a time. Add ground nuts, fruits and grated citrus rind. Reserve whole blanched almonds for top of cake. Batter will be stiff.

Grease and flour a deep 8-inch round springform pan. Spread the batter in pan. Top with whole almonds, arranged in circles. Bake cake in preheated 350° oven for about 1 1/4 to 1 1/2 hours, or until tester inserted in center of cake comes out clean. Cool 5 minutes on wire rack.

CHOCOLATE WALNUT ZUCCHINI CAKE — **Sharon Kline**

3 eggs
2 c. sugar
1 c. oil
2 oz. unsweetened chocolate
1 tsp. vanilla
2 c. grated zucchini
3 c. flour
1 tsp. cinnamon
1 tsp. salt
1/4 tsp. baking powder
1 tsp. baking soda
1 c. chopped walnuts

Beat eggs, beat in sugar and oil. Melt chocolate, stir into egg mixture along with vanilla and zucchini.

Mix dry ingredients together and then add all at once to batter. Mix thoroughly.

Spoon into greased 9 x 13 or 2 (8 x 8) baking pans. Bake 1 hour at 350° for 9 x 13 pan. Sprinkle with 10X sugar when slightly cooled.

WALNUT BUTTER BALLS — **Mrs. Sam Gladwin**

2 c. finely chopped walnuts
2 c. flour
1 c. butter or margarine, softened
1/2 c. granulated sugar
2 tsp. vanilla
1/4 tsp. salt
confectioners sugar

Chop walnuts, then combine with flour, butter, granulated sugar, vanilla and salt. Mix with fork or hands until well blended. With lightly floured hands shape into 1-inch balls and bake on ungreased cookie sheet in 325° oven for 20 minutes, or till browned on bottom. Let cool slightly before removing from sheet.

Let cool, then shake cookies in confectioners sugar, a few at a time, till coated.

Makes about 5 dozen.

BLENDER CHEESE CAKE

Mrs. Sam Gladwin

3/4 c. milk
2 tsp. vanilla
2 eggs
1 c. sugar
1/2 c. Bisquick
2 (8 oz.) pkgs. cream cheese

Topping:

1 c. sour cream
2 tsp. sugar
1/2 tsp. vanilla

Blend milk, vanilla, eggs, sugar and Bisquick on high for 15 seconds. Add 2 packages cream cheese, a little at a time, to blender contents and blend 2 minutes on high.

Pour into a greased deep dish pie plate. Bake at 350° for 40-45 minutes. Let cool.

Topping: Mix sour cream, sugar and vanilla and spread over top of cheese cake, serve cool.

AUNT LOUISE'S WEDDING CAKE

Kris Leonard

2 c. sugar
1 c. Crisco
4 eggs
2 c. plain flour
1/2 c. self-rising flour
1 tsp. vanilla
1 c. milk

Cream sugar and Crisco. Add eggs, 1 at a time. Add milk, vanilla. Sift together flours, add to sugar mix; blend well.

Bake at 325° for 1 hour in tube pan.

To bake in layers, bake larger layers 45-60 minutes; smaller check at 30 minutes.

Use toothpick to check for doneness. Make sure cake is done before taking from oven.

CREAMY RICE PUDDING

Sherry Heward

1/2 c. uncooked rice
1/4 c. sugar
1/4 tsp. nutmeg
1/4 tsp. vanilla extract
1 qt. milk

1. Combine rice, sugar and nutmeg. Stir in raisins and milk.
2. Cover and bake at 350° for 2 hours, stirring occasionally. Uncover and bake 30 minutes longer, allowing a skin to form.
3. Cool and serve warm or cold.

STOLLEN

Jenny Moody

1-2 c. raisins and 1 1/2 c. candied fruit <u>or</u> 2-3 c. raisins
5 c. flour
1 pkg. dry active yeast
1/2 tsp. salt
3/4 c. sugar
1 c. milk
cinnamon
1/2 c. butter
2 eggs
1 tsp. vanilla
8-12 oz. slivered almonds/pecans
1/4 c. butter, melted
confectioner's sugar
brown sugar

In large bowl, mix yeast, 1 cup flour, salt and 3/4 cup sugar. Heat milk and butter until milk is very warm (120°-130°F.), do not boil. Beat milk into flour mixture for 2 minutes.

Add eggs, vanilla and 1 cup flour. Beat for 2 more minutes. Add enough flour to make soft dough. Turn out on generously floured board and knead for 5-10 minutes (until dough is smooth and elastic). Place dough in lightly greased bowl. Cover and let rise in warm place until double, about 2 hours.

Punch dough down. Turn out onto floured board and gently knead in fruits, raisins. Divide dough in half. Roll 1/2 into a rectangle (at least 8 x 12 inches or 10 x 14 inches), about 1/2-inch thick. Brush with melted butter. Sprinkle with cinnamon and brown sugar generously. Cover with nuts. Fold about 1/3 of dough to center. Repeat with other side, overlapping about 1 inch. Place on greased baking sheet. Mold stollen by tapering ends to form an oval. Repeat process with second loaf.

Brush tops with melted butter. Let rise until double, about 1 hour.

Bake in preheated oven at 375° for about 25 minutes, until golden brown and crusty. (Watch carefully.)

When cool, cover with confectioner's sugar, sifted is prettiest and eat. This reheats nicely and quickly.

CINNAMON CAKE

Linda Murphy

1 c. sugar
1 Tbsp. shortening
1 egg
2 c. flour
2 1/2 tsp. baking powder
1 c. milk
3/4 c. sugar
cinnamon to brown sugar

Mix all but last sugar and cinnamon. Put in greased 8- or 9-inch square pan. Dot with butter or margarine. Mix sugar and cinnamon and sprinkle on top of cake.

Bake at 350° for 25-30 minutes.

AUNT FRANCES' CHOCOLATE CAKE

Kris Leonard

1 stick butter
1 c. water
3 squares chocolate
2 c. sugar
2 eggs
2 c. plain or cake flour
1 tsp. baking soda
1/2 tsp. baking powder
1 c. sour cream

Bring to boil: butter, water and chocolate; set aside to cool. When cool, beat in remaining ingredients in order listed. Sift together flour and baking soda and baking powder before adding. If using plain flour add 1/4 teaspoon salt.

Bake at 350° in 8- or 9-inch layers until done. (Test at 30 minutes.)

Frosting:

2 c. sugar
1/4 c. Karo syrup
1/2 c. milk
1 stick butter
1/4 tsp. salt
3 squares chocolate

Stir over low heat until chocolate is melted, bring to boil for 1 minute. Remove from heat and beat until lukewarm, then stir in 1 teaspoon vanilla. Continue beating until it's the right consistency to spread.

SURPRISE MERINGUES

Kris Leonard

2 egg whites
1/8 tsp. salt
1/8 tsp. cream of tartar
1 tsp. vanilla
3/4 c. sugar
1 (6 oz.) pkg. chocolate chips
1/4 c. chopped walnuts

Beat egg whites, salt, cream of tartar and vanilla until soft peaks form. Add sugar gradually, beat until stiff peaks form - do not overbeat. Fold in chocolate and nuts.

Cover cookie sheet with plain paper or lightly spray with Pam. Drop mixture by rounded teaspoonfuls onto cookie sheet.

Bake at 300° for 25 minutes. Makes about 2 dozen.

CHOCOLATE CHIP COOKIES

Madeline Nelson
(Kris Miller's Mom)

1 box yellow cake mix
1/3 c. vegetable oil
1 tsp. vanilla
2 eggs
1 (6 oz.) pkg. semi-sweet chocolate chips
1/2 c. chopped nuts

Heat oven to 375°. Mix about 1/2 of the cake mix, the vegetable oil, vanilla and eggs in large bowl until smooth. Stir in remaining cake mix, the chocolate chips and nuts.

Drop dough by teaspoonfuls about 2 inches apart onto ungreased cookie sheet. Bake 10 to 12 minutes. Centers will be soft. Cool slightly; remove from cookie sheet.

5 dozen cookies.

ECLAIR CAKE

Linda Murphy

2 pkgs. instant French vanilla pudding
3 c. milk
1 (8 oz.) container Cool Whip
graham crackers
1 can chocolate icing

Mix 2 packages pudding with 3 cups milk as per directions on package. Add 8 ounces Cool Whip to pudding, mix well. Layer graham crackers on bottom of 9 x 13-inch pan. Put 1/2 pudding on crackers, layer of crackers, rest of pudding and top with layer of graham crackers. Put chocolate icing on top (it helps to soften icing in microwave). Refrigerate.

FESTIVE FRUITCAKE

Madeline Nelson
(Kris Miller's Mom)

2 eggs
2 c. water
2 pkgs. Pillsbury date or nut quick bread mix
2 c. pecans (halves or chopped)
2 c. raisins
3 (8 oz.) pkgs. or 3 c. candied fruit (red cherries, green cherries, natural pineapple, orange peel and citron)
corn syrup

Heat oven to 350°. Grease and flour bottom and sides of tube pan.

In large bowl, combine eggs and water. Add remaining ingredients except corn syrup, stir by hand until combined. Pour into pan.

Bake at 350°F. for 75 to 85 minutes or until toothpick inserted in center comes out clean. Cool in pan 30 minutes; loosen edges and remove from pan. Cool completely. Wrap in plastic wrap or foil and store in refrigerator. Glaze with warm corn syrup before serving.

STRAWBERRY ANGEL FOOD CAKE

Madeline Nelson
(Kris Miller's Mom)

1 baked angel food cake
1 (3 oz.) pkg. strawberry jello
1 c. hot water
10 oz. frozen sliced strawberries
2 c. whipped cream
whole strawberries for garnish

Thaw berries. Dissolve jello in hot water and add berries. Chill until partially set. Fold in 1 cup whipped cream. Chill until thick.

Cut cake crosswise into 3 layers. Put strawberry mixture between layers and frost cake with 1 cup of whipped cream and garnish with whole berries.

MILK CHOCOLATE FROSTING

Madeline Nelson
(Kris Miller's Mom)

3 Tbsp. butter or margarine
2 Tbsp. cocoa
1 1/2 c. confectioners sugar
2 Tbsp. milk
1 tsp. vanilla

Melt 3 tablespoons butter in a medium saucepan. Stir in 2 tablespoons cocoa until dissolved. Add 1 1/2 cups confectioners sugar, 2 tablespoons milk, 1 teaspoon vanilla. Stir until smooth. Add more milk if necessary to make a soft spreading consistency. Frost brownies, let set until firm.

DUMP CAKE

Madeline Nelson
(Kris Miller's Mom)

1 cake mix
1 can crushed pineapple in syrup (undrained)
1 (21 oz.) can cherry pie filling
1 c. chopped pecans
1/2 c. (1 stick) margarine, cut in slices

Preheat oven to 350°. Grease 13 x 9 x 2 pan.

Dump undrained pineapple into pan; spread evenly. Dump in pie filling and spread into even layer. Dump dry cake mix onto cherry layer, spread evenly. Sprinkle pecans over cake mix. Put mixture over top.

Bake at 350° for 50 to 55 minutes. Serve warm or cooled.

MARBLED BROWNIES

Madeline Nelson
(Kris Miller's Mom)

1 box family-size brownie mix (Duncan Hines)
2 (3 oz.) pkgs. cream cheese
5 Tbsp. margarine
1/3 c. sugar
5 eggs (total in recipe)
2 Tbsp. flour
3/4 tsp. vanilla

Cream Cheese Mixture: Soften cream cheese and margarine, beat together. Add sugar, 2 eggs, flour and vanilla; beat until smooth, set aside.

Brownie Batter: Empty brownie mix and chocolate flavor packet into medium-size bowl. Add 2 tablespoons water and 3 eggs. Mix by hand about 50 strokes.

Pour half the brownie batter into a greased 13 x 9-inch pan. Spoon the cream cheese mixture over the brownie layer. Use remaining brownie batter here and there over the cream cheese batter. Pull knife through batter in wide curves to create a swirled appearance.

Bake at 350° for 35-40 minutes. Cool and frost.

WHITE FROSTING

Kris Miller

2 egg whites
1/3 c. water
1 c. sugar
1/8 tsp. cream of tartar
1 tsp. vanilla
1/8 tsp. salt

Heat sugar and water in a saucepan over low heat. Beat rest of ingredients in glass mixing bowl at high speed. Mixture will be foamy, continue to beat at high speed gradually adding melted sugar and water. Frosting will thicken and form peaks. (Takes approximately 15 to 20 minutes to stiffen and form peaks.) Frost on your favorite cake.

*This frosting cannot be refrigerated, nor can cake after iced with this frosting or icing will "run". Best results if beaters and mixing bowl are cold. Put in the freezer for 5 minutes before using.

*Variation: Try 1 to 2 drops of food coloring (any color) for beautiful colored icing. Beat an additional 1 to 2 minutes, or 1 to 2 drops of strawberry extract or extract of your choice.

CHOCOLATE CREAM FILLED ANGEL FOOD CAKE

Madeline Nelson (Kris Miller's Mom)

1 box angel food cake mix
1 (4 serving size) pkg. chocolate instant pudding mix
1 1/2 c. cold milk
1 box whipped topping mix (2 envelopes)

Mix, bake and cool cake as directed on the cake mix box. After placing cake on a serving plate, slice a 1-inch layer from the top and set aside.

Cut around cake 1-inch from outer edge, down to 1 inch from bottom. Then cut around cake 1 inch from inner edge down to 1 inch from bottom. Gently pull out the cake between the cuts leaving a 1 inch layer on the bottom; tear removed cake into small pieces.

In a medium-size mixing bowl, combine pudding mix, 1 envelope whipped topping mix and 1 1/2 cups milk. Whip mixture until it becomes thick, but not stiff, 2-3 minutes.

Fold cake pieces into whipped mixture. Put in cake shell evenly. Replace top of cake. Prepare remaining whipped topping envelope as package directed. Spread over sides and top of cake. Chill cake for 1/2 hour before serving to allow filling to set. Makes 12 to 16 servings.

HUMMINGBIRD CAKE

Kris Miller

3 c. flour
2 c. sugar
1 tsp. soda
1 tsp. salt
1 tsp. cinnamon
3 eggs, beaten
1 1/2 c. vegetable oil
1 c. chopped nuts
2 c. chopped bananas
8 oz. can crushed pineapple (save juice)

Grease and flour a 10-inch tube pan.

In large bowl, combine flour, sugar, soda, salt and cinnamon. Add remaining ingredients and stir until mixed (hand mixed only). Pour into pan, bake 1 hour 10 minutes. Cool on rack. This cake is very good plain or frost with icing below.

Icing for Hummingbird Cake:

8 oz. soft cream cheese
1 stick butter (soft)
1 tsp. vanilla
1 box powdered sugar

Beat cheese, butter and vanilla till light. Add sugar slowly and continue to mix. Spread over cake.

SPICY CARROT CAKE

Kris Miller

1 1/2 c. vegetable oil
2 1/2 c. sugar
4 eggs, separated
2 1/2 c. sifted all-purpose flour
1/4 tsp. salt
1 1/2 tsp. baking powder
1/2 tsp. baking soda
1 c. pecans, chopped
1/2 tsp. nutmeg
1 tsp. ground cloves
1 tsp. cinnamon
1 3/4 c. raw carrots, grated and divided

Preheat oven to 350°F. Grease and flour 10-inch tube cake pan.

Mix oil and sugar together. Beat in egg yolks, one at a time, continue to beat and add 5 tablespoons of hot water. Sift together flour, baking powder, baking soda, salt and spices. Add to egg mixture. Reserve 1/4 cup of grated carrots for garnish and stir in remaining carrots and pecans. Fold in beaten egg whites.

Pour batter into pan and bake at 350° for 60 to 70 minutes. Cool in pan for 15 minutes, then turn over on cake rack to finish cooling. Drizzle glaze (below) in a circle on the top of the cake and sprinkle with reserved grated carrots.

Glaze:

3 Tbsp. lemon juice
3/4 c. powdered sugar

Mix together. Use to top carrot cake (above).

HOT MILK CAKE

Madeline Nelson
(Kris Miller's Mom)

2 c. sugar
4 eggs
1 c. milk
1 stick margarine
1 tsp. vanilla
2 c. flour
1 tsp. baking powder

Beat eggs and sugar in a large bowl. Heat milk and margarine in a saucepan until margarine is nearly melted. DO NOT BOIL. Pour hot milk into sugar and egg mixture. Add vanilla and stir, then add flour and baking powder. Blend well. Pour into greased bundt pan.

Bake at 375° for 35 to 45 minutes.

HONEY-SWEETENED ALL NATURAL CARROT CAKE

Kris Leonard

1 1/2 c. oil
3/4 c. honey
3 eggs
3 c. unbleached flour
1 tsp. soda
1 tsp. each: cinnamon, nutmeg
1/2 tsp. ground cloves
2 c. grated carrots
1 (10 oz.) can crushed unsweetened pineapple and juice
1 1/2 c. unsweetened coconut flakes
1 c. chopped walnuts
1 c. raisins

Cream together oil, honey and eggs. Add flour, soda, spices, carrots, pineapple, juice and coconut and mix well. Stir in walnuts and raisins.

Pour into a greased bundt pan or 2 (9-inch) cake pans. Bake at 325° for 50 minutes.

Cream Cheese Frosting:

1 (8 oz.) pkg. cream cheese
1/4 c. butter
3 Tbsp. honey
1 tsp. vanilla extract

Cream together - if it needs thinning use milk or plain yogurt.

MINIATURE CHEESE CAKES

Shirley Necessary

24 cupcake liners
24 vanilla wafers
2 (8 oz.) pkgs. cream cheese, softened
3/4 c. sugar
2 eggs
1 Tbsp. lemon juice
1 tsp. vanilla
1 (20 to 21 oz.) can Comstock cherries or blueberry filling
1/2 c. sliced nuts (optional)

Line cupcake pans with liners. Place a vanilla wafer in bottom of each liner.

In small bowl, beat cream cheese, sugar, eggs, lemon juice and vanilla until light and fluffy. Fill the liners 2/3 full with cheese mixture.

Bake in preheated oven at 375° for 15 to 20 minutes, or until set. Top each with a spoonful of filling and 1 teaspoon nuts. Chill.

Serves 24.

NO BAKE COOKIES

Madeline Nelson (Kris Miller's Mom)

1 c. sugar
2 tsp. cocoa
1/2 stick butter
1/4 c. cold milk
1/2 tsp. vanilla
1/4 c. peanut butter
1 1/2 c. rolled oats

Measure first 4 ingredients into a 1 1/2-quart saucepan and bring to a rolling boil for 1 minute.

Stir in vanilla, peanut butter and oats. Drop onto wax paper by the teaspoon. Cool 10 minutes.

CHEESECAKE

Kris Miller

1 box yellow cake mix (reserve 1 c.)
3 Tbsp. oil
4 eggs
1 1/2 c. milk
1 Tbsp. vanilla
3 Tbsp. lemon juice
2 (8 oz.) pkgs. cream cheese
1/2 c. sugar

Crust: Blend cake mix (minus 1 cup), 3 tablespoons oil and 1 egg. Spread in bottom of pan.

Filling: Combine 2 (8-ounce) packages cream cheese and cream with 1/2 cup sugar. Add 3 eggs, 1 cup remaining cake mix. Gradually add 1 1/2 cups milk, 3 tablespoons lemon juice, 1 tablespoon vanilla.

Pour filling from bowl onto crust. Bake at 325° for 50 to 55 minutes. Serve as is or top with cherry or other flavored pie filling.

DUMP CAKE

Shirley Necessary

1 can Comstock cherries or blueberries
1 small box Washington's yellow cake mix
butter
walnuts

In small casserole dish (glass meat loaf pan works great). Put cherries, then sprinkle dry cake mix over top, then pads of butter, then walnuts.

Bake 30 minutes on 350°.

HAWAIIAN PINEAPPLE UPSIDE-DOWN CAKE

Nancy Dove

1 (1 lb. 4 1/2 oz.) can sliced or crushed pineapple
maraschino cherries
1/4 c. butter or margarine
1/2 c. firmly packed brown sugar
1 (1 layer) yellow cake mix

Drain pineapple well. Melt butter or margarine in 9-inch round cake pan. Remove from heat and stir in brown sugar.

Arrange pineapple and cherries in sugar mixture. Prepare cake mix (as directed on package) and pour over all in pan.

Bake at 350° for 40 or 50 minutes until wooden pick inserted in center comes out clean. Loosen edges of cake, cover with serving plate, turn over and lift off pan.

Serves 8 or 9.

BANANA SPLIT CAKE

Sharon Hale

10X sugar
2 eggs
margarine
bananas
crushed pineapple
Cool Whip
graham cracker crumbs

Take 2 cups graham cracker crumbs and 1 stick of margarine, melted. Mix together, then pat to make a bottom crust in a 9 x 13 pan.

Now, mix your butter creme layer by mixing 2 cups 10X sugar, 2 eggs, 1 cup margarine and beat 15 minutes (15 minutes a must to get right consistency). Spread half of the butter creme over crust, then slice 4 bananas in little circles over top of the butter creme layer.

Now make a second butter cream layer with the other half. Drain 1 (16-ounce) can of crushed pineapple and spread out, then finally top it off with 16 ounces of Cool Whip. Tastes best when refrigerated at least 1 hour.

Write an extra recipe here:

CANDY • JELLY
JAM • PRESERVES

Candy & Frosting Chart

230 degrees - 234 degrees	Thread
234 degrees - 240 degrees	Soft Ball
244 degrees - 248 degrees	Firm Ball
250 degrees - 266 degrees	Hard Ball
270 degrees - 290 degrees	Soft Crack
300 degrees - 310 degrees	Hard Crack

Birthdays

Monday's child is fair of face,
Tuesday's child is full of grace,
Wednesday's child is loving and giving,
Thursday's child works hard for a living,
Friday's child is full of woe,
Saturday's child has far to go,
But the child that is born on the Sabbath day
Is brave and bonny, and good and gay.

PERPETUAL CALENDAR

SHOWING THE DAY OF THE WEEK FOR ANY DATE BETWEEN 1700 AND 2499

Table of Dominical Letters

Year of the Century (* Denote Leap-Years)				Centuries 1700, 2100	1800, 2200	1900, 2300	2000, 2400
0	*28	*56	*84	C	E	G	A
1	29	57	85	B	D	F	G
2	30	58	86	A	C	E	F
3	31	59	87	G	B	D	E
*4	*32	*60	*88	E	G	B	C
5	33	61	89	D	F	A	B
6	34	62	90	C	E	G	A
7	35	63	91	B	D	F	G
*8	*36	*64	*92	G	B	D	E
9	37	65	93	F	A	C	D
10	38	66	94	E	G	B	C
11	39	67	95	D	F	A	B
*12	*40	*68	*96	B	D	F	G
13	41	69	97	A	C	E	F
14	42	70	98	G	B	D	E
15	43	71	99	F	A	C	D
*16	*44	*72		D	F	A	B
17	45	73		C	E	G	A
18	46	74		B	D	F	G
19	47	75		A	C	E	F
*20	*48	*76		F	A	C	D
21	49	77		E	G	B	C
22	50	78		D	F	A	B
23	51	79		C	E	G	A
*24	*52	*80		A	C	E	F
25	53	81		G	B	D	E
26	54	82		F	A	C	D
27	55	83		E	G	B	C

Month					Dominical Letter						
January, October					A	B	C	D	E	F	G
Feb., Mar., Nov.					D	E	F	G	A	B	C
Jan., Apr., July					G	A	B	C	D	E	F
May					B	C	D	E	F	G	A
June					E	F	G	A	B	C	D
February, August					C	D	E	F	G	A	B
Sept., Dec.					F	G	A	B	C	D	E
1	8	15	22	29	Su	Sa	F	Th	W	Tu	M
2	9	16	23	30	M	Su	Sa	F	Th	W	Tu
3	10	17	24	31	Tu	M	Su	Sa	F	Th	W
4	11	18	25		W	Tu	M	Su	Sa	F	Th
5	12	19	26		Th	W	Tu	M	Su	Sa	F
6	13	20	27		F	Th	W	Tu	M	Su	Sa
7	14	21	28		Sa	F	Th	W	Tu	M	Su

EXPLANATION

Find first the *Year of the Century* and in line with that figure at the right, in the proper column under the heading *Centuries,* will be found the Dominical Letter of the year. Then in the table headed *Dominical Letter* and in line with the proper ***Month*** find the letter previously determined. Run down this column until you are in line with the proper Day of the Month and at the intersection you will find the Day of the Week.

In Leap-Years the Dominical Letters for January and February will be found in the lines where these months are printed in *italics*.

EXAMPLES

On what day of the week did January 5, 1891, fall? For 1891 the Dominical Letter is "D." After finding this letter opposite January in the upper right hand table, and running down that column until you are opposite 5 (the day of the month), you will find Monday. For *January* 1, 1876, the Dominical Letter is "A." Under "A," and in line with 1 is Saturday.

27 MINUTE APPLE BUTTER

Bonnie Swecker

8 c. applesauce
5 c. sugar
1/2 c. vinegar
1/2 c. cinnamon hearts
5 tsp. ground cinnamon

Mix ingredients all together and stir. Cook (27 minutes). Seal in jars.

PEANUT BUTTER FUDGE

Gail Price

2/3 c. evaporated milk
1/2 tsp. vanilla
1/2 stick butter
2 1/2 c. sugar
1 heaping c. mini marshmallows
1 c. peanut butter

In medium saucepan, over low heat, bring to boil: evaporated milk, sugar and butter. Start timer, boil 10 minutes. Leaving saucepan on heat, add marshmallows, peanut butter and vanilla, stirring well.

Turn out into buttered 9 x 9-inch pan. Allow to cool 1 to 2 hours before slicing.

ESTHER'S FUDGE - 1973

Portia Morris

3 c. white sugar
1 1/3 c. evaporated milk
1 stick margarine
1/2 tsp. salt
about 50 marshmallows (more or less)

Bring to full boil, stirring constantly, over medium heat and boil 5 minutes.

Remove from heat and stir in:

2 tsp. vanilla
20 oz. pkg. chocolate chips
2 c. walnuts

Pour in 9 x 11 pan. Makes approximately 4 1/2 pounds.

CHOCOLATE FUDGE — Bonnie Swecker

Easy. Makes about 3 pounds.

3 (6 oz.) pkgs. semi-sweet chocolate chips
1 (14 oz.) can Eagle Brand sweetened condensed milk
dash salt
1/2 to 1 c. chopped nuts (walnuts)
1 1/2 tsp. vanilla extract

In heavy saucepan, over low heat, melt chips with milk and salt. Remove from heat. Stir in nuts and vanilla. Spread evenly into wax paper-lined 8- or 9-inch pan. Chill 2 hours or until firm. Peel off wax paper, cut and store loosely.

DOUBLE CHOCOLATE FANTASY BARS — Bonnie Swecker

1 (18 1/4 or 18 1/2 oz.) pkg. chocolate cake mix
1/3 vegetable oil
1 egg
1 c. chopped nuts
1 (14 oz.) Eagle Brand sweetened condensed milk
1 (6 oz.) pkg. semi-sweet chocolate chips
1 tsp. vanilla
dash salt

Makes 36 bars. Preheat oven to 350°. Bake 25 to 30 minutes or until bubbly. Cool, cut into bars, covered at room temperature.

In large mixing bowl, beat cake mix, oil and egg on medium speed until crumbly. Add nuts. Reserving 1 1/2 cups crumb mixture, press remainder firmly on bottom of greased 13 x 9-inch baking pan.

In small saucepan, combine remaining ingredients over medium heat. Cook and stir until chips melt. Pour evenly over prepared crust. Top with reserved crumb mixture.

APPLESAUCE — Madeline Nelson (Kris Miller's Mom)

1/2 c. boiling water
2 lbs. cooking apples, peeled, cored and sliced
1/8 tsp. ground cinnamon
1/8 ground cloves
1/2 c. sugar

Place all ingredients in heavy saucepan. Cook over medium heat until the desired doneness is reached, about 20 to 30 minutes simmering time. The apples variety will determine how long the cooking time will take.

RAISIN HONEY CHEWS
Kris Leonard

1 1/2 c. shortening
1 3/4 honey
2 eggs
1 tsp. grated orange peel
2 1/2-3 c. flour
1 tsp. salt
4-5 c. oats
2 c. raisins

Cream together shortening, honey, eggs and orange peel, stir in dry ingredients, add raisins.

Drop by tablespoonfuls onto greased baking sheets. Bake at 375° for 8-10 minutes.

CHOCOLATE COVERED CHERRIES
Kris Leonard

For Fondant:

2 lbs. confectioners sugar
1/4 lb. margarine
1 large can sweetened condensed milk
2 tsp. vanilla
1 large jar maraschino cherries

Mix and chill fondant ingredients (except cherries) overnight, roll into balls with cherries in center, chill again.

1 large bar semi-sweet (or milk) chocolate
1/2 bar paraffin (if desired)

Melt together in double boiler. Dip cherries in chocolate. Cool on wax paper, store in refrigerator.

HOMEMADE PEANUT BUTTER
Bobbi Dorsey

1 lb. shelled peanuts
1/2 to 1 tsp. salt
1/2 to 1 tsp. sugar
2 Tbsp. peanut oil

In a food processor or blender process half the nuts, salt, sugar and oil to a creamy consistency. Empty into a bowl. Repeat with remaining.

Refrigerated, keeps about 1 month. Makes about 1 3/4 cups.

For chunky - coarsely chop one third of the nuts and add to the rest of processed ingredients.

MINT MERINGUES

Misty Frye

2 egg whites
1/2 tsp. cream of tartar
pinch salt
3/4 c. sugar
3 drops green food coloring
1 (10 oz.) bag mint chocolate chips

Preheat oven to 375° for at least 15 minutes.

Beat egg whites, salt and cream of tartar until peaks form. Add sugar gradually, 1/4 cup at a time, continue beating until stiff. Add coloring with last addition of sugar. Fold chocolate chips in by hand.

Cover a cookie sheet with wax paper and drop 1/2 teaspoon mounds of mixture on it. Turn oven off and put candy in. Leave in until candy is thoroughly dried out.

OLD FASHION FUDGE

Gail Frye

3 c. sugar
2/3 c. cocoa
1 tsp. salt
2 c. milk
2 tsp. vanilla extract
1 stick butter
1 c. peanut butter or 1 c. chopped walnuts (optional)

Combine sugar, cocoa and salt. Mix very well. Add milk. Mix well. Bring to boil on high heat. Reduce to medium heat until it starts to thicken and lose some of its glaze (soft ball stage). Add extract, butter and optional ingredients. Remove from heat. Stir by hand until mixture starts to harden.

Pour into buttered platter. Chill for 15 minutes, cut into squares and serve.

Write an extra recipe here:

BEVERAGES
MISCELLANEOUS

For Pensive Moments

A word of advice - do not give it.

Love thy enemies - it will drive them nuts.

To share with a friend is to see twice the beauty.

The recipe that is not shared with others will soon be forgotten, but when it is shared, it will be enjoyed by future generations.

There is nothing wrong with the younger generations that twenty years will not cure.

The flower that follows the sun, does so even on cloudy days.

A loose tongue often gets into a tight place.

One mother can care for five children, but five children cannot care for one mother.

A neighbor asked a small boy if his family said prayers before the meals. "No," he replied, "We don't have to. My mother is a good cook".

People who expect the worst, usually find it.

Even a mosquito does not get a slap on the back until he starts working.

Always do right - this will gratify some people and astonish the rest.

Happiness is like potato salad - when you share it with others, it is a picnic.

Remember when health foods were whatever your mother said to eat - or else?

Be careful how you live - you may be the only Bible some people read.

I can keep a secret, but those I tell it to never can.

Delicious food that melts in your mouth also sticks to your hips.

The most difficult meal for the average housewife is to get dinner out.

Even worse than a storm or a riot is a bunch of kids who are suddenly quiet.

One should never question his wife's judgement - after all, she married him.

Good judgement comes from experience. Experience comes from bad judgement.

It takes a clever man to know how to agree with his wife in such a way that she will change her mind.

HOLIDAY PUNCH

Linda Cole

cranberry juice cocktail
pale dry ginger ale
1 qt. vanilla ice cream (approximately)
fruit (optional) your choice - pineapple chunks, orange, lemon or lime slices, etc.

In a large punch bowl, pour equal amounts of cranberry juice cocktail and ginger ale.

Drop in small scoops of vanilla ice cream. Float fruit sections on top of punch if desired.

Serve in small punch glasses.

NEW ENGLAND INDIAN PUDDING

Portia Morris

(My favorite)

1/2 c. yellow cornmeal
1 qt. milk (scalded)
2/3 c. molasses
1 tsp. salt
2 c. cold milk

Add cornmeal slowly to hot milk, stirring constantly, over boiling water until thick. Add molasses and salt.

Pour into greased baking dish and add cold milk. Bake in slow oven (275°) 3 hours. Serve hot with whipped cream, ice cream or hard sauce.

Variations:

Spicy: Use 1/2 teaspoon each of cinnamon and ginger.

Apple: Pare and slice 2 apples. Place in alternate layers with pudding mixture before baking. Use spice or not as desired.

Note: This pudding is very popular in many New England homes and fine Inns. It dates back to the 1600's when the Pilgrims landed at Plymouth, Massachusetts.

MOCK CHAMPAGNE PUNCH

Misty Frye

1 (6 oz.) can lemonade concentrate
1 (6 oz.) can pineapple concentrate
3 c. cold water
1 (28 oz.) bottle ginger ale, chilled
1 (25 oz.) bottle sparkling white grape juice, chilled

In a punch bowl, combine lemonade and pineapple concentrates with water. Stir until dissolved. Stir in ginger ale and grape juice. Serve over ice.

CRAB IMPERIAL

Gail Frye

1/2 c. mayonnaise
1 beaten egg
2 Tbsp. chopped pimento
1 Tbsp. chopped green onion
1 1/2 tsp. Worcestershire sauce
1 tsp. lemon juice
1 tsp. dry mustard
dash hot pepper sauce
1 lb. crabmeat
black pepper to taste and paprika

Combine mayonnaise, egg, pimento, onion, Worcestershire sauce, lemon juice, mustard and hot sauce. Mix well. Gently stir in crabmeat.

Spoon into individual casserole dishes or scallop shells. Sprinkle with paprika. Microwave on HIGH power 7-9 minutes, rearranging dishes once.

Makes 4-6 servings.

CHICKEN ASPARAGUS ROLLS

Linda Murphy

1/4 tsp. garlic powder
1/4 tsp. rosemary
1/2 tsp. salt (optional)
2 whole boneless chicken breasts, halved, skin removed, pounded to flatten
2 (1 oz.) slices Mozzarella cheese, halved
1 (10 oz.) pkg. frozen asparagus spears, defrosted, drained
1/4 tsp. paprika
2 tsp. grated Parmesan cheese

Serves 4 - 245 calories each.

In small bowl, combine garlic powder, rosemary and salt. Sprinkle over chicken. Lay 1/2 slice cheese on each piece. Top with 4 asparagus spears. Fold long edges of chicken breast over asparagus; secure with wooden toothpick. Sprinkle chicken rolls on all sides with paprika.

Place seam down in 12 x 8-inch baking dish. Cover with wax paper. Microwave at HIGH 3 minutes. Turn and rearrange chicken pieces. Sprinkle with Parmesan; cover. Microwave on HIGH 2-4 minutes or until chicken is opaque and tender.

BROCCOLI CASSEROLE

Bobbi Dorsey

1 (1 lb. approximate) bag frozen broccoli cuts
1 (8 oz.) jar Cheez Whiz
1 can cream of celery soup
1/2 stick margarine
2 c. (or more) cooked rice

Mix together Cheez Whiz, soup and melted margarine. Add to rice and broccoli and bake at 350° about 20 minutes, or until bubbly and broccoli is tender.

(Very easy.)

MICROWAVE SCALLOPED POTATOES

Bobbi Dorsey

3 Tbsp. margarine or butter
1/4 c. flour
1 3/4 c. chicken broth
1/4 c. mayonnaise
2 1/2 lbs. potatoes, peeled and sliced thin
1 medium-size onion, sliced thin

Melt margarine or butter in a shallow 2-quart microwave-safe baking dish. Stir in flour until smooth, then gradually add broth until blended. Microwave, uncovered, on HIGH 4 to 4 1/2 minutes until thick, whisking once. Stir in mayonnaise. Gently stir in potatoes and onion to coat. Cover with lid or vented plastic wrap.

Microwave on HIGH 16 to 18 minutes, rotating dish 1/4 turn twice, until potatoes in center are almost tender when pierced. Let sit a few minutes before serving.

GRANOLA NUT BARS

Nancy Dove

1 (6 oz.) pkg. semi-sweet chocolate pieces
1 Tbsp. peanut butter
1 1/2 c. granola with coconut and nuts
1/2 c. wheat flakes cereal
1/2 c. chopped dates
1/2 c. raisins

Combine chocolate and peanut butter in 2-quart measure. Use cook cyle and cook 3 to 4 minutes, or until chocolate is melted. Stir until smooth. Add remaining ingredients and stir until thoroughly coated. Drop by teaspoonful onto wax paper. Chill until firm.

FROSTY FRUIT CUP

Misty Frye

1 (15 oz.) can pineapple chunks in juice
1 (16 oz.) bottle diet lemon-lime soda
2 Tbsp. lime juice
1 c. seedless green grapes
green food coloring

Drain pineapple, save juice. Combine juice, soda, lime juice and food coloring; stir. Freeze to a mush about 2-2 1/2 hours. Combine fruits. Break frozen mixture apart with a fork. Spoon into dessert glasses. Top with fruit mixture.

Makes 8 servings, 66 calories per serving.

RED FRUIT PUNCH

Barbara Shanahan

1 can red Hawaiian Punch
2 qts. ginger ale
frozen orange juice ring with cherries and orange slices frozen in it

Pour into large punch bowl - 1 can Hawaiian Punch to 2 quarts of ginger ale. Stir, put frozen orange juice ring with cherries and orange slices frozen in it on top.

This ring will float, as it melts it keeps the punch cold and releases the fruit and tastes great.

You can increase 2 or 3 times with the same ring and it still tastes great.

Write your extra recipes here:

Basic Kitchen Information

THUMB INDEX

Expression of Appreciation

For their help and cooperation in providing this indexed, up-to-date, authentic information of basic value to our book, our organization and the sponsors wish to thank the helpful institutions, businesses, Governmental agencies and the home economists who worked on it.

National Live Stock and Meat Board.

U.S. Department of Agriculture.

Armour and Co.

Wheat Flour Institute.

EQUIVALENTS

3 tsps.	1 tbsp.
4 tbsps.	¼ cup
5⅓ tbsps.	⅓ cup
8 tbsps.	½ cup
10⅔ tbsps.	⅔ cup
12 tbsps.	¾ cup
16 tbsps.	1 cup
½ cup	1 gill
2 cups	1 pt.
4 cups	1 qt.
4 qts.	1 gal.
8 qts.	1 peck
4 pecks	1 bu.
16 ozs.	1 lb.
32 ozs.	1 qt.
8 ozs. liquid	1 cup
1 oz. liquid	2 tbsps.

(For liquid and dry measurements use standard measuring spoons and cups. All measurements are level.)

WEIGHTS AND MEASURES

Baking powder
1 cup = 5½ ozs.

Cheese, American
1 lb. = 2⅔ cups cubed

Cocoa
1 lb = 4 cups ground

Coffee
1 lb. = 5 cups ground

Corn meal
1 lb. = 3 cups

Cornstarch
1 lb. = 3 cups

Cracker crumbs
23 soda crackers = 1 cup
15 graham crackers = 1 cup

Eggs
1 egg = 4 tbsps. liquid
4 to 5 whole = 1 cup
7 to 9 whites = 1 cup
12 to 14 yolks = 1 cup

Flour
1 lb. all-purpose = 4 cups
1 lb. cake = 4½ cups
1 lb. graham = 3½ cups

Lemons, juice
1 medium = 2 to 3 tbsps.
5 to 8 medium = 1 cup

Lemons, rind
1 lemon = 1 tbsp. grated

Oranges, juice
1 medium = 2 to 3 tbsps.
3 to 4 medium = 1 cup

Oranges, rind
1 = 2 tbsps. grated

Gelatin
3¼ oz. pkg. flavored = ½ cup
¼ oz. pkg. unflavored = 1 tbsp.

Shortening or Butter
1 lb. = 2 cups

Sugar
1 lb. brown = 2½ cups
1 lb. cube = 96 to 160 cubes
1 lb. granulated = 2 cups
1 lb. powdered = 3½ cups

To Remove STAINS From Washables

ALCOHOLIC BEVERAGES
Pre-soak or sponge fresh stains immediately with cold water, then with cold water and glycerine. Rinse with vinegar for a few seconds if stain remains. These stains may turn brown with age. If wine stain remains, rub with concentrated detergent; wait 15 min.; rinse. Repeat if necessary. Wash with detergent in hottest water safe for fabric.

BLOOD
Pre-soak in cold or warm water at least 30 minutes. If stain remains, soak in lukewarm ammonia water (3 tablespoons ammonia per gallon water). Rinse. If stain remains, work in detergent, and wash, using bleach safe for fabric.

CANDLE WAX
Use a dull knife to scrape off as much wax as possible. Place fabric between two blotters or facial tissues and press with warm iron. Remove color stain with non-flammable dry cleaning solvent. Wash with detergent in the hottest water safe for fabric.

CHEWING GUM
Rub area with ice, then scrape off with dull blade. Sponge with dry cleaning solvent; allow to air dry. Wash in detergent and hottest water safe for fabric.

CHOCOLATE AND COCOA
Pre-soak stain in cold or warm water. Wash in hot water with detergent. Remove any grease stains with dry cleaning solvent. If color remains, sponge with hydrogen peroxide, wash again.

COFFEE
Sponge or soak with cold water as soon as possible. Wash, using detergent and bleach safe for fabric. Remove cream grease stain with non-flammable dry cleaning solvent. Wash again.

CRAYON
Scrape with dull blade. Wash in hottest water safe for fabric, with detergent and 1-2 cups of baking soda.

NOTE: If full load is crayon stained, take to cleaners or coin-op dry cleaning machines.

DEODORANTS
Sponge area with white vinegar. If stain remains, soak with denatured alcohol. Wash with detergent in hottest water safe for fabric.

DYE
If dye transfers from a non-colorfast item during washing, immediately bleach discolored items. Repeat as necessary BEFORE drying. On whites use color remover.

CAUTION: Do not use color remover in washer, or around washer and dryer as it may damage the finish.

To Remove STAINS From Washables

EGG
Scrape with dull blade. Pre-soak in cold or warm water for at least 30 minutes. Remove grease with dry cleaning solvent. Wash in hottest water safe for fabric, with detergent.

FRUIT AND FRUIT JUICES
Sponge with cold water. Pre-soak in cold or warm water for at least 30 minutes. Wash with detergent and bleach safe for fabric.

GRASS
Pre-soak in cold water for at least 30 minutes. Rinse. Pre-treat with detergent. Wash, using detergent, hot water, and bleach safe for fabric. On acetate and colored fabrics, use 1 part of alcohol to 2 parts water.

GREASE, OIL, TAR
Method 1: Use powder or chalk absorbents to remove as much grease as possible. Pre-treat with detergent or non-flammable dry cleaning solvent, or liquid shampoo. Wash in hottest water safe for fabric, using plenty of detergent.
Method 2: Rub spot with lard and sponge with a non-flammable dry cleaning solvent. Wash in hottest water and detergent safe for fabric.

INK--BALL-POINT PEN
Pour denatured alcohol through stain. Rub in petroleum jelly. Sponge with non-flammable dry cleaning solvent. Soak in detergent solution. Wash with detergent and bleach safe for fabric.

INK--FOUNTAIN PEN
Run cold water through stain until no more color will come out. Rub in lemon juice and detergent. Let stand 5 minutes. Wash.
If a yellow stain remains, use a commercial rust remover or oxalic acid, as for rust stains.
CAUTION: HANDLE POISONOUS RUST REMOVERS CAREFULLY. KEEP OUT OF REACH OF CHILDREN. NEVER USE OXALIC ACID OR ANY RUST REMOVER AROUND WASHER AND DRYER AS IT CAN DAMAGE THE FINISH. SUCH CHEMICALS MAY ALSO REMOVE PERMANENT PRESS FABRIC FINISHES.

LIPSTICK
Loosen stain with a non-flammable dry cleaning solvent. Rub detergent in until stain outline is gone. Wash in hottest water and detergent safe for fabric.

MEAT JUICES
Scrape with dull blade. Pre-soak in cold or warm water for 30 minutes. Wash with detergent and bleach safe for fabric.

MILDEW
Pre-treat as soon as possible with detergent. Wash. If any stain remains, sponge with lemon juice and salt. Dry in sun. Wash, using hottest water, detergent and bleach safe for fabric.
NOTE: Mildew is very hard to remove; treat promptly.

To Remove STAINS From Washables

MILK, CREAM, ICE CREAM
Pre-soak in cold or warm water for 30 minutes. Wash. Sponge any grease spots with non-flammable dry cleaning solvent. Wash again.

NAIL POLISH
Sponge with polish remover or banana oil. Wash. If stain remains, sponge with denatured alcohol to which a few drops of ammonia have been added. Wash again. Do not use polish remover on acetate or triacetate fabrics.

PAINT
-oil base
Sponge stains with turpentine, cleaning fluid or paint remover. Pre-treat and wash in hot water. For old stains, sponge with banana oil and then with non-flammable dry cleaning solvent. Wash again.
-water base
Scrape off paint with dull blade. Wash with detergent in water as hot as is safe for fabric.

PERSPIRATION
Sponge fresh stain with ammonia; old stain with vinegar. Pre-soak in cold or warm water. Rinse. Wash in hottest water safe for fabric. If fabric is yellowed, use bleach. If stain still remains, dampen and sprinkle with meat tenderizer, or pepsin. Let stand 1 hour. Brush off and wash. For persistent odor, sponge with colorless mouthwash.

RUST
Soak in lemon juice and salt or oxalic solution (3 tablespoons oxalic acid to 1 pint warm water). A commercial rust remover may be used.
CAUTION: HANDLE POISONOUS RUST REMOVERS CAREFULLY. KEEP OUT OF REACH OF CHILDREN. NEVER USE OXALIC ACID OR ANY RUST REMOVER AROUND WASHER OR DRYER AS IT CAN DAMAGE THE FINISH. SUCH CHEMICALS MAY ALSO REMOVE PERMANENT PRESS FABRIC FINISHES.

SCORCH
Wash with detergent and bleach safe for fabric. On heavier scorching, cover stain with cloth dampened with hydrogen peroxide. Cover this with dry cloth and press with hot iron. Rinse well.
CAUTION: Severe scorching cannot be removed because of fabric damage.

SOFT DRINKS
Sponge immediately with cold water and alcohol. Heat and detergent may set stain.

TEA
Sponge or soak with cold water as soon as possible. Wash using detergent and bleach safe for fabric.

PARTY PLANNING

Buffet Setting

A buffet makes it easy to serve a large group in a small dining area. This setting can be used for any meal by just placing the food in the order of your menu, plates first and eating utensils last.

1. Plates; 2. Main dish;
3. Gravy boat on liner plate;
4. Vegetable dish;
5. Other side dish;
6. Salad bowl; 7. Relish tray; 8. Basket of rolls;
9. Napkins with knives, fork and spoons;
10. Salt and pepper;
11. Centerpiece and candles.

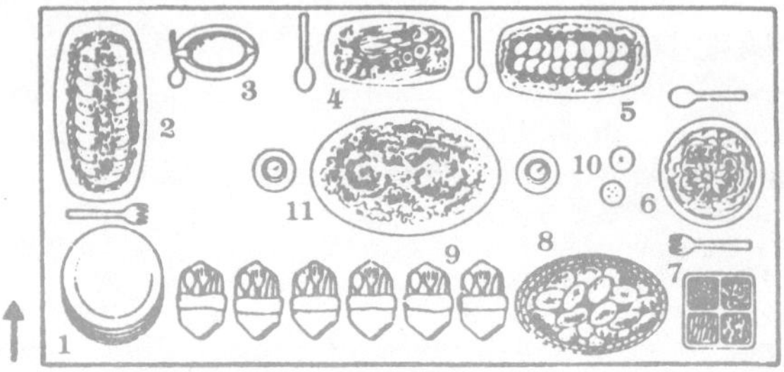

Luncheon

A luncheon can be great fun no matter what size the crowd. An optional fruit or soup first course could be followed by:

1. Hot casserole or omelet, bread and a light dessert.
2. Cold combination salad, bread and a rich dessert.
3. Small salad, hot main dish and dessert.

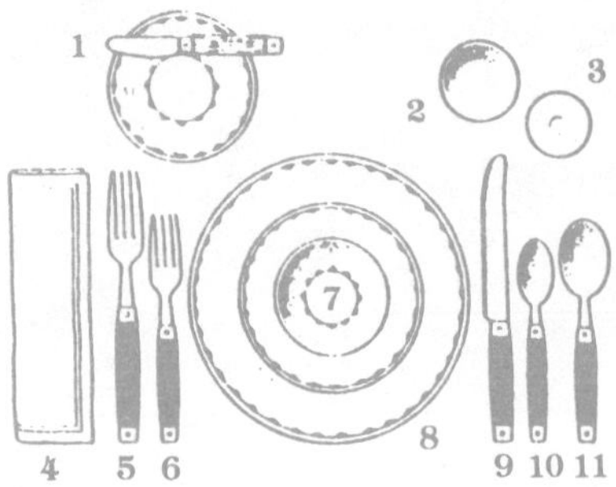

1. Bread and butter plate and knife; 2. Water glass; 3. Optional drink glass; 4. Napkin; 5. Luncheon fork; 6. Dessert fork; 7. First course bowl and liner plate; 8. Luncheon plate; 9. Knife; 10. Teaspoon; 11. Soup spoon.

Dinner

You don't have to wait for a special occasion to have a formal dinner party. Sunday dinners with family and friends is a wonderful reason to celebrate by serving a formal dinner and it will almost guarantee help with the extra dishes!

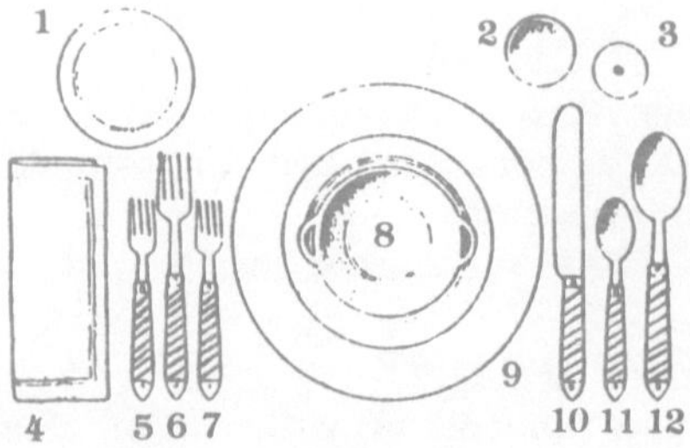

1. Salad plate; 2. Water glass; 3. Optional drink glass; 4. Napkin; 5. Salad fork; 6. Dinner fork; 7. Dessert fork; 8. First-course bowl and liner plate; 9. Dinner plate; 10. Dinner knife; 11. Teaspoon; 12. Soup spoon.

PARTY PLANNING

Napkin Folding

Add a final decorative touch to your dinner table by folding napkins into any of the shapes below. Napkins may also be placed on the dinner plates.

BUTTERFLY

Form a triangle from an open napkin. Fold the right corner to the center.

Take the left corner up to center, making a diamond. Keeping the loose points at the top, turn the napkin over, then fold upward, to form a triangle.

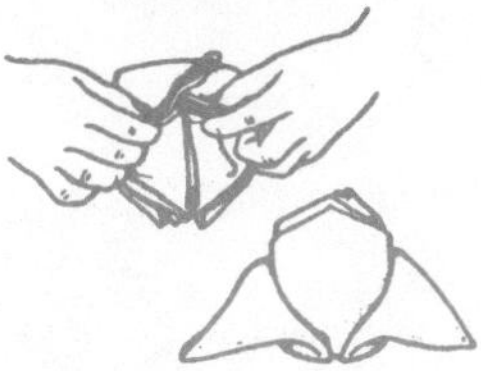

Tuck the left corner into the right. Stand up napkin; turn it round, then turn the petals down; it's now a butterfly.

ARTICHOKE

Place all 4 points to the center of an opened napkin.

Fold the 4 points to the center of the napkin once more.

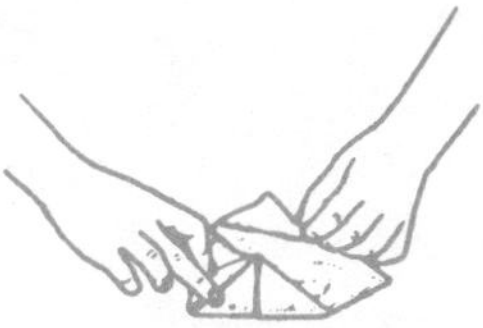

Repeat a third time; turn napkin over and fold points to the center once more.

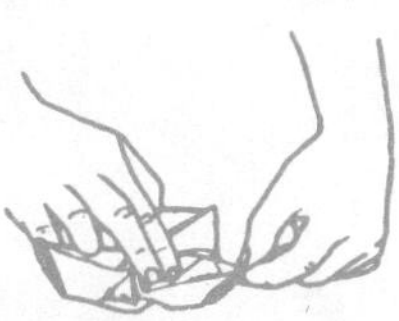

Holding finger firmly at center, unfold 1 petal first from underneath each corner.

Pull out 4 more from between the petals. Then pull out the next 4 under the petals.

The artichoke now has 12 points.

SILVER BUFFET

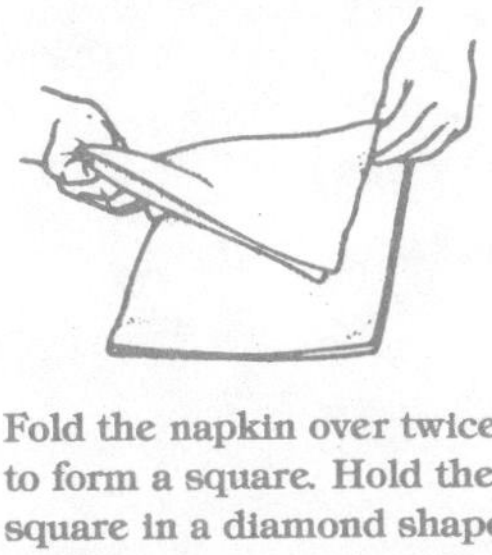

Fold the napkin over twice to form a square. Hold the square in a diamond shape.

Take the top 2 flaps and roll them halfway down the napkin.

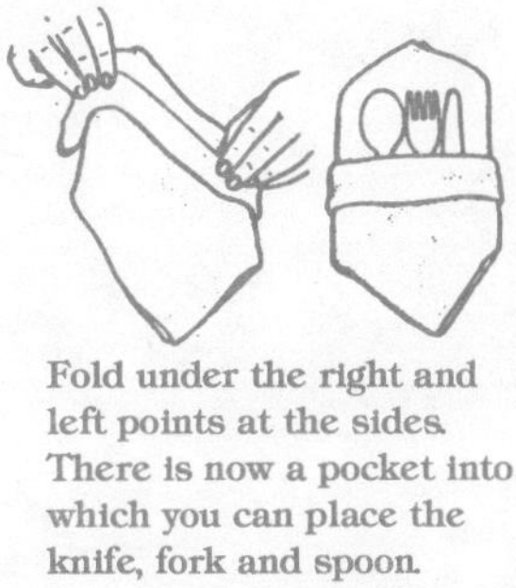

Fold under the right and left points at the sides. There is now a pocket into which you can place the knife, fork and spoon.

6 Easy Steps

TO THE

1 The ingredients for the perfect pie crust: 1 teaspoon salt, 2/3 cup vegetable shortening. 2 cups flour, and cold water.

2 Cut shortening into flour and salt mixture with a fork or pastry blender until crumbs are coarse and granular.

3 Add 3 to 6 tablespoons cold water, a little at a time. Mix quickly and evenly through the flour until the dough just holds together.

Perfect Pie

4 Roll half the dough to about one-eighth inch thickness. Lift edge of pastry cloth and roll crust onto rolling pin. Line pie pan, allowing one-half inch crust to extend over edge.

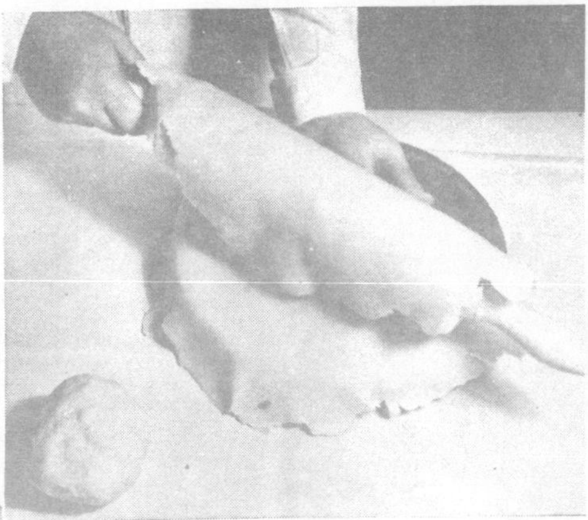

5 Add filling. Roll out top crust, making several gashes to allow escape of steam. Place over filling. Allow top crust to overlap lower crust. Fold top crust under the lower and crimp edges.

6 And here is the perfect pie, baked in a moderately hot oven (425° F.) for thirty-five minutes.

TIME TABLE FOR MEAT COOKERY

Broiling

CUT	THICKNESS	WEIGHT RANGE	APPROXIMATE TOTAL TIME (MINUTES)		
			RARE	MEDIUM	WELL DONE
BEEF					
Rib Steak	1 inch	1-1½ lb.	8-10	12-14	18-20
Club Steak	1 inch	1-1½ lb.	8-10	12-14	18-20
Porterhouse	1 inch	1½-2 lbs.	10-12	14-16	20-25
	1½ inch	2½-3 lbs.	14-16	18-20	25-30
	2 inch	3-3½ lbs.	20-25	30-35	40-45
Sirloin	1 inch	2½-3½ lbs.	10-12	14-16	20-25
	1½ inch	3½-4½ lbs.	14-16	18-20	25-30
	2 inch	5-5½ lbs.	20-25	30-35	40-45
Ground Beef Patties	¾ inch	4 oz. each	8	12	15
Tenderloin	1 inch		8-10	12-14	18-20
LAMB					
Rib or Loin					
Chops (1 rib)	¾ inch	2-3 oz. each	—	—	14-15
Double Rib	1½ inch	4-5 oz. each	—	—	22-25
Lamb Shoulder Chops	¾ inch	3-4 oz. each	—	—	14-15
	1½ inch	5-6 oz. each	—	—	22-25
Lamb Patties	¾ inch	4 oz. each	—	—	14-15
HAM, BACON & SAUSAGE					
Ham Slices	½ inch	9-12 oz. each	—	—	10-12
	¾ inch	1-1¼ lb.	—	—	13-14
	1 inch	1¼-1¾ lbs.	—	—	18-20
Bacon					4-5
Pork Sausage Links		12-16 to the lb.	—	—	12-15
Broiling Chickens (drawn) halves		1-1½ lbs.	—	—	30-35

Stewing

CUT	WEIGHT RANGE	APPROXIMATE TIME
Beef—1-1½ inch cubes from neck, chuck, plate or heel of round	2 lbs.	2½-3 hours
Veal or Lamb 1-1½ inch cubes from shoulder or breast	2 lbs.	1½-2 hours
Chicken	3½-4 lbs.	2-2½ hours

Simmering in Water

CUT	WEIGHT RANGE	APPROXIMATE TIME
Fresh Beef Brisket or Plate	8 lbs.	4-5 hours total
Corned Beef Brisket half or whole	4-8 lbs.	4-6 hours total
Cross Cut Shanks of Beef	4 lbs.	3-4 hours total
Fresh or Smoked Beef Tongue	3-4 lbs.	3-4 hours total
Pork Hocks	3/4 lbs.	3 hours total
Whole Ham	12-16 lbs.	18-20 min. per lb.
Ham Shanks	5-6 lbs.	25-30 min. per lb.
Smoked Pork Butt (boneless)	2-3 lbs.	40 min. per lb.
Picnic	7-8 lbs.	35-40 min. per lb.
Chicken	3½-4 lbs.	2-2½ hours total

TIME TABLE FOR MEAT COOKERY

Roasting

CUT	WEIGHT RANGE	COOKING TEMP.	INTERNAL MEAT TEMP.	APPROXIMATE TIME
BEEF				
Standing Ribs (3)	6-8 lbs.	325° F.		
Rare			140° F.	16-18 min. per lb.
Medium			160° F.	20-22 min. per lb.
Well Done			170° F.	25-30 min. per lb.
Rolled Rib	5-7 lbs.	325° F.		Add 10-12 min. per lb. to above time
Rump-boneless	5-7 lbs.	325° F.	170° F.	30 min. per lb.
VEAL				
Leg (center, cut)	7-8 lbs.	325° F.	170° F.	25 min. per lb.
Loin	4½-5 lbs.	325° F.	170° F.	30-35 min. per lb.
Rack 4-6 ribs	2½-3 lbs.	325° F.	170° F.	30-35 min. per lb.
Shoulder-bone-in	6-7 lbs.	325° F.	170° F.	25 min. per lb.
Shoulder Boneless Roll	5-6 lbs.	325° F.	170° F.	35-40 min. per lb.
LAMB				
Leg	6-7 lbs.	325° F.	175-180° F.	30-35 min. per lb.
Shoulder Bone-in	5-7 lbs.	325° F.	175-180° F.	30-35 min. per lb.
Shoulder Boneless Roll	4-6 lbs.	325° F.	175-180° F.	40-45 min. per lb.
FRESH PORK				
Loin	4-5 lbs.	350° F.	185° F.	30-35 min. per lb.
Cushion Shoulder	4-6 lbs.	350° F.	185° F.	35-40 min. per lb.
Shoulder Boned & Rolled	4-6 lbs.	350° F.	185° F.	40-45 min. per lb.
Shoulder Butt	4-6 lbs.	350° F.	185° F.	45-50 min. per lb.
Fresh Ham	10-14 lbs.	350° F.	185° F.	30-35 min. per lb.
Spare Ribs (1 side)	1½-2½ lbs.	350° F.	185° F.	1-1½ hrs. total
SMOKED PORK				
Ham—whole	10-12 lbs.	325° F.	150-155° F.	18-20 min. per lb.
	14-16 lbs.	325° F.	150-155° F.	16-18 min. per lb.
Ham-half	6-8 lbs.	325° F.	150-155° F.	25-27 min. per lb.
Ham—2 inch slice	2½-3 lbs.	325° F.	170° F.	1½ hrs. total
Picnic	5-8 lbs.	325° F.	170° F.	33-35 min. per lb.
POULTRY				
Chickens stuffed weight	4-5 lbs.	325° F.	185° F.	35-40 min. per lb.
Chickens over 5 lbs.		325° F.	185° F.	20-25 min. per lb.
Turkeys stuffed weight	6-10 lbs.	325° F.	185° F.	20-25 min. per lb.
Turkey	10-16 lbs.	325° F.	185° F.	18-20 min. per lb.
Turkey	18-25 lb	325° F.	185° F.	15-18 min. per lb.

Geese—Same as turkey of similar weight.
Duck—Same as heavy chicken of similar weight.

Braising

CUT	WEIGHT RANGE	APPROXIMATE TIME
Beef Pot Roast, Chuck, Rump or Heel of Round	3-5 lbs.	Brown then simmer 3½-4 hours
Swiss Steak (round) 1 in. thick	2 lbs.	Brown then simmer 1½-2 hours
Flank Steak	1½-2 lbs.	Brown then simmer 1½ hours
Beef Short Ribs	2-2½ lbs.	Brown then simmer 2-2½ hours
Ox Tails	1-1½ lbs.	Brown then simmer 3-4 hours
Rolled Lamb Shoulder Pot Roast	3-5 lbs.	Brown then simmer 2-2½ hours
Lamb Shoulder Chops	4-5 oz. each	Brown then simmer 35-40 min.
Lamb Neck Slices	½ lb. each	Brown then simmer 1-1½ hours
Lamb Shanks	1 lb. each	Brown then simmer 1½ hours
Pork Rib or Loin Chops	4-5 oz. each (¾-1 inch)	Brown then simmer 35-40 min.
Pork Shoulder Steaks	5-6 oz. each	Brown then simmer 35-40 min.
Veal Rolled Shoulder		
Pot Roast	4-5½ lbs.	Brown then simmer 2-2½ hours
Cutlets or Round	2 lbs.	Brown then simmer 45-50 min.
Loin or Rib Chops	3-5 oz. each	Brown then simmer 45-50 min.

Freezing Prepared Foods

PACKAGING MATERIALS

Materials used for packaging foods for freezing should keep the air out and the moisture in so select containers that are moisture-vapor resistant or the food will dry out.

Waxed papers, household aluminum foil, and cartons for cottage cheese and ice cream are *not suitable*, because they are *not* moisture-vapor-resistant.

Select a *size* that will hold enough vegetable or fruit for a meal for your family.

Select containers that pack easily into a little space.

Consider cost of containers and if they are re-useable, or not. If they are reuseable, a high initial cost may be justified.

Rigid containers are made of aluminum, glass, plastic, tin or heavily waxed cardboard. They can be used for vegetables, fruits, cooked foods or liquids.

Non-Rigid containers-as sheets and bags of cellophane, heavy aluminum foil, plastic film, polyethylene, or laminated paper are used for foods that are firm but irregulaly shaped, like poultry, meat, and baked goods.

Bags are generally used inside cartons as moisture resistant liners.

There is no economy in using poor quality packaging materials.

Fill packages carefully, allowing for the necessary head space for the particular kind of food.

Force or draw out as much air as possible, seal tightly, label, freeze immediately, and store at 0° F or lower.

Foods should be frozen in amounts which will ordinarily be eaten in one meal. To treat light colored fruits to prevent darkening, use ascorbic acid. When freezing fruit in sugar syrup, add ½ teaspoon ascorbic acid for each quart syrup. When freezing fruit in dry sugar, sprinkle ascorbic acid dissolved in water over fruit before adding sugar. Use ¼ teaspoon ascorbic acid in ¼ cup cold water to each quart of fruit.

Freezing Prepared Foods May Not Save Time. It May Allow Time To Be Used To Better Advantage.

GENERAL INFORMATION

Prepare the dish as if it were to be served right away, but do not cook quite done. Reheating for serving will finish the cooking.

Cheese or crumb toppings are best added when the food is reheated for serving.

Pastry crumbs frozen unbaked are more tender, and flaky, and have a fresher flavor than those baked and then frozen.

Cool the cooked food quickly. Pour out in shallow pans or place the uncovered pan of food in iced or very cold water; change water to keep it cold.

As soon as the food is cool-60°F or less, pack promptly into moisture-vapor-resistant containers or packaging material. Pack tightly to force out as much air as possible.

To have the food in desired amounts for serving and for quicker defrosting, separate servings with 2 pieces freezer paper.

Since many main dishes are semi-liquid it is desirable to pack them in rigid containers. Foods frozen in containers with wide-mouthed openings do not have to be thawed completely to remove from container.

Some main dishes may be frozen in the containers in which they were baked.

Freezer weight foil (.0015 gauge) may be used to line the baking dish or pan. After the main dish is frozen (unwrapped) in this container, remove from the baking dish and package. The food may be reheated by slipping it and the foil into the baking pan.

Allow head space for freezing liquid and semi-liquid foods. Seal; label; freeze quickly and store at 0° F or lower.

Most precooked, frozen, main dishes are reheated, either in the oven or on top of the range. Reheating in the oven takes little attention and usually preserves the texture of the food better. Reheating on top of the range in a double boiler or a sauce pan is faster. When using a double boiler, start with warm, not hot, water in the lower pan so the food won't stick. Food reheated over direct heat needs to be stirred. This stirring may give a less desirable texture.

If partial thawing is necessary, before the food can be removed from the package, place in luke warm water for a few minutes. Complete thawing should be done in the refrigerator. If it takes more than 3 or 4 hours, thawing at room temperature may cause dangerous spoilage.

It is best to freeze meat pies and turnovers unbaked.

You can use any good meat loaf recipe for freezing. Just make enough for several meals instead of one and freeze the extra loaves.

Nuts are likely to discolor and become bitter when frozen in a salad mixture.

Suggested Maximum Home-Storage periods To Maintain Good Quality in Purchased Frozen Foods

Food	Approximate holding period at 0° F.
Fruits and vegetables	Months
Fruits:	
Cherries	12
Peaches	12
Raspberries	12
Strawberries	12
Fruit juice concentrates:	
Apple	12
Grape	12
Orange	12
Vegetables:	
Asparagus	8
Beans	8
Cauliflower	8
Corn	8
Peas	8
Spinach	8
Baked gooas	
Bread and yeast rolls:	
White bread	3
Cinnamon rolls	2
Plain rolls	3
Cakes:	
Angel	2
Chiffon	2
Chocolate layer	4
Fruit	12
Pound	6
Yellow	6
Danish pastry	3
Doughnuts:	
Cake type	3
Yeast raised	3
Pies (unbaked):	
Apple	8
Boysenberry	8
Cherry	8
Peach	8
Meat	
Beef:	
Hamburger or chipped (thin) steaks	4
Roasts	12
Steaks	12
Lamb:	
Patties (ground meat)	4
Roasts	9
Pork, cured	2
Pork, fresh:	
Chops	4
Roasts	8
Sausage	2
Veal:	
Cutlets, chops	9
Roasts	9
Meat - Continued	Months
Cooked meat:	
Meat dinners	3
Meat pie	3
Swiss steak	3
Poultry	
Chicken:	
Cut-up	9
Livers	3
Whole	12
Duck, whole	6
Goose, whole	6
Turkey:	
Cut-up	6
Whole	12
Cooked chicken and turkey:	
Chicken or turkey dinners (sliced meat and gravy)	6
Chicken or turkey pies	6
Fried chicken	4
Fried chicken dinners	4
Fish and shellfish	
Fish:	
Fillets:	
Cod, flounder, haddock, halibut, pollack	6
Mullet, ocean perch, sea trout, striped bass	3
Pacific Ocean perch	2
Salmon steaks	2
Sea trout, dressed	3
Striped bass, dressed	3
Whiting, drawn	4
Shellfish:	
Clams, shucked	3
Crabmeat:	
Dungeness	3
King	10
Oysters, shucked	4
Shrimp	12
Cooked fish and shelfish:	
Fish with cheese sauce	3
Fish with lemon butter sauce	3
Fried fish dinner	3
Fried fish sticks, scallops, or shrimp	3
Shrimp creole	3
Tuna pie	3
Frozen desserts	
Ice cream	1
Sherbet	1

EVERY DAY HERB GUIDE

	ANISE SEED	BASIL	BAY LEAVES	CARAWAY SEED	DILL SEED	OREGANO	ROSEMARY	SAGE	SESAME SEED	TARRAGON	THYME	TURMERIC
APPETIZERS & BEVERAGES	Adds licorice flavor to Milk or Tea	Pizza, Stuffed Celery, Butter Spreads, Tomato Juice	Tomato and Vegetable Juices	Add whole to Popcorn Balls, Cheese Spreads & Dips, Tea	Use ¼ tsp. in Spreads, Avocado Dip, a dash in Tomato Juice	Pizza, Guacamole, Sharp Cheese Spread, Vegetable & Tomato Juice	Gin Punch	Sharp Cheese Spreads, Tea	Add to Dips and Spreads. Sprinkle toasted seed over Canapes	Avocado Dip, Liver Pate, Vegetable & Tomato Juices	Fish Spreads, Clam & Tomato Juices	
BREADS & ROLLS	Use as garnish or add to dough for Coffeecake and Sweet Rolls			Biscuits, Waffles, Rye Bread, Rolls	Rye and Dark Breads	Herb Bread	Biscuits, Corn Bread	Biscuits, Corn Bread, Waffles	Use generously in Biscuits, Buns, Coffee-cake, Waffles Breads		Biscuits	
CAKES & COOKIES	Add whole or crushed to Spongecake, Spicecake, Cupcakes			Delightful addition to Poundcake, Spicecake	Use crushed in Poundcake				Cheesecake			
CASSEROLES	An unusual touch in Stew	Crush leaves just before adding to Goulash, Stews, Veal Scaloppine, Meat Pies, Spanish Rice, Stuffing	All Stews, Chicken Casseroles & Rice Dishes	Meat Pie Crusts, Stews, Noodle Dishes	Lamb Stew, Macaroni, Chicken Dishes. Use ¼ to ½ tsp. per 4 servings	Use ⅛ tsp. for 6 servings, crushed, in Chili Con Carne, Tamale Pie, Beef & Veal Stew	Use ¼ tsp. per 4 servings, crushed, in Corned Beef & Cabbage, Ham Loaf, Chicken Stew, BeefStew, Dumplings	Use ¼ tsp. pcr 4 servings in Stews, Cheese Casseroles, Stuffings & Dumplings	Dumplings, Crumb Toppings, Rice Dishes	Use ¼ tsp. per 4 servings in Chicken A La King, Cheese Casseroles	Use ½ tsp. for 4 servings, crushed, in Stews, Chipped Beef, Creamed Chicken, Croquettes, Fricassees	Macaroni & Noodle Dishes. Rice Dishes where Saffron is not used, Curried Dishes,
DESSERTS	Springerle, Butter Cookies, Candies, All Fruit Pies, Compotes, Applesauce, Stewed Apples			Use crushed or whole in Rolled Cookies & Candies, Baked & Stewed Apples	Rolled "Dilly Cookies, Apple Pie				Rolled Cookies, Pastries, Pecan Pie, Piecrusts			Rolled Cookies
EGGS & CHEESE	Cottage & Cream Cheese	Scrambled Eggs, Souffles, Rarebits, Cream & Cottage Cheese		Cottage Cheese, Rarebits	Omelets, Egg Dishes, Cottage & Cream Cheese	Scrambled Eggs, Omelets	Omelets, Deviled & Scrambled Eggs	Creamed Eggs, Cheddar & Cottage Cheese	Soft Cheeses	Omelets, Eggs Benedict, All Egg Dishes, Cottage Cheese	Shirred Eggs, Cottage Cheese	Sprinkle on Souffles, Creamed, Deviled & Scrambled Eggs

FISH	Hard-Shelled Crab, Shrimp, Steamed Cod	Shrimp, Lobster, Halibut	Cod, Boiled or Steamed Shrimp, Crab & Lobster, Poached Halibut & Salmon	Clams, Oysters, Shrimp	Halibut, Shrimp, Sole, Lobster	Shrimp, Clams, Lobster, Stuffed Fish	Salmon, Crab, Shrimp, Halibut, Creamed Seafood	Baked Halibut, Salmon, Cod	Sprinkle on Fish before broiling, or add to breading	Crab, Lobster, Salmon, Tuna	Sprinkle lightly on Tuna, Scallops, Crab, Sole, Clams	Creamed Salmon, Lobster, Shrimp
MEAT & POULTRY	Use ¼ tsp. for 4 servings of Veal, Chicken, Duck, Sausage	Veal Roast, Lamb Chops, Liver, Barbecued Chicken, Duck, Sausage	Pot Roast, Oxtails, Shish Kebab, Sauerbraten, Boiled Pork or Chicken	Spareribs, Roast Pork, Liver, Kidneys, Goose	Beef, Veal, Pork Chops, Lamb Chops	Meatloaf, Meatballs, Pork, Veal, Swiss Steak, Duck, Lamb, Sausage, Stuffings	Beef, Pork, Veal, Lamb, Poultry, Game	All Pork Dishes, Duck, Hamburgers, Sausage, Meat Loaf	Pork Chops, Chicken Cutlets, Lamb, add 2 tsp. to 1 lb. ground beef for hamburgers	Broiled Chicken, Squab, Duck, Steaks, Veal	All Meats, Meatloaf, Liver, Chicken, Turkey	Add ⅛ tsp. to Curried Lamb or Beef, Broiled Chicken
PRESERVES & PICKLES	Add whole to Sweet Pickles	Mustard Sauce	Beets, Mixed & Sour Pickles	Beets, Sour & Mixed Pickles	Dill Pickles, of course!	Mustard Sauce		Mustard Sauce		Mustard Sauce, Sour Pickles	Mustard Sauce	Chow Chow, Chutney, Mixed Pickles, Relishes
SALADS & DRESSINGS	Use whole or crushed in Waldorf, Fruit and Vegetable Salads	Aspics, Tossed, Chicken, Seafood & Cucumber Salads, French & Russian Dressings	Aspics, Tomato Salad, French Dressing	Add whole to Potato, Vegetable, Tomato & Cucumber Salads, Cole Slaw, Dressings	Potato, Macaroni, Cucumber & Vegetable Salads, French & Sour Cream Dressings	Egg, Bean, Tomato, Vegetable, Seafood Salads	Fruit or Meat Salads	Salad Greens & French Dressing	Vegetable Salads & Dressings	Tossed, Chicken, Fruit, Seafood, Egg Salads, Dressings & Vinegars	Tossed, Beet & Tomato Salads, Tomato Aspic	Use ½ tsp. per cup in French & Mayonnaise Dressings, or ¼ tsp. for color
SAUCES & GRAVIES		Seafood, Butter, Spaghetti, Tomato & Pizza Sauces	Bordelaise & Marinades	Marinades, Seasoned Butters	Crush and add to Cream Sauce, Spiced Vinegar, Drawn Butter	Spaghetti, Tomato, Cream, Butter Sauces, Marinades & Gravies	Cheese, A La King, Barbecue Spaghetti & Tomato Sauces, Brown Gravy	Add a dash to Brown & Cream Gravies, Barbecue Sauce		Bearnaise, Butter, Mustard, Tartar, Sweet-Sour Sauces, Marinades	Bordelaise, Creole, Butter & Barbecue Sauces	Add ¼ tsp. to Butter, Cheese, Cream & Mustard Sauces
SOUPS & CHOWDERS		Bean, Beef, Pea, Tomato, Potato, Turtle, Manhattan Clam Chowder	Vegetable, Bean, Fish Chowders	Creamed, Fish Bisques	Chicken, Cream of Tomato, Split Pea, Navy Bean	Bean, Beef, Minestrone, Tomato Soups & Fish Chowder	Chicken, Minestrone, Split Pea, Vegetable	Creamed, Fish, Chicken Chowder, Consomme	Creamed Soups	Chicken, Consomme, Mushroom, Fish, Pea, Tomato	Gumbo, Fish & Clam, Pea, Vegetable	Add a dash to Creamed Soups and Chowders
VEGETABLES		Eggplant, Peas, Squash, String Beans, Zucchini; perfect for all Tomatoes	Asparagus, Beets, Beans, Carrots, Artichokes, Boiled Potatoes, Tomatoes	Asparagus, Cauliflower, French Fried Potatoes, Cabbage, Sauerkraut	Add ¼ tsp. to Beets, Carrots, Peas, Cabbage, Turnips, Cauliflower, Sauerkraut, Tomatoes	Onions, Potatoes, Peas, Spinach, String Beans, Tomatoes, Zucchini	Eggplant, Beans, Peas, Squash, Spinach, Boiled Potatoes, Sauteed Mushrooms	Green Beans, Eggplant, Brussels Sprouts, Onions, Lima Beans, Peas, Tomatoes	Use toasted as garnish for Asparagus, Boiled Potatoes, Green Beans, Tomatoes, Spinach	Asparagus, Beans, Broccoli, Cabbage, Peas, Cauliflower, Mushrooms, Potatoes, Tomatoes	Artichokes, Beans, Beets, Carrots, Mushrooms, Onions, Tomatoes, Potatoes	Sprinkle on Creamed Potatoes

A DIET TO LIVE WITH

Good nutrition is important whether you are dieting to lose weight or to maintain your ideal weight. A good low-calorie diet meets your daily nutritional needs, subtracting calories without sacrificing the minerals, vitamins and other food requirements. With the lists below you can keep your diet varied and exciting. It is imperative that you combine choices from each of the groups daily.

GROUP I: DARK GREEN AND YELLOW VEGETABLES

These vegetables are high in essential minerals-iron, calcium and phosphorus- and in vitamins A and C. A one cup serving of the starred (*) vegetables will supply all the vitamin A you need daily. Using two or more of the other vegetables listed will round out your daily nutritional needs. This does not include butter or margarine. Those calories are counted from Group IX.

35 calories per ½ cup serving:

* Carrots * Pumpkin * Winter squash (butternut, acorn or hubbard)

20 calories per ½ cup serving:

Asparagus (6 spears)	Broccoli	* Spinach	Green Beans
Green Peppers	* Kale	* Dandelion Greens	Tomatoes
Turnip Greens	* Collards	* Mustard Greens	

* Escarole and Lettuce equal 15 calories in a one cup serving.

GROUP II: OTHER VEGETABLES

These vegetables are also important for daily nutritional needs. Plan one or more servings per day and do not substitute with vegetables in Group I. These vegetables do not include butter or margarine. Those calories are counted from Group IX.

50 calories for ½ cup serving:

Beets Onions Parsnips Turnips (¾ cup)

15 calories or less per ½ cup serving:

Bean Sprouts	Brussel Sprouts	Cabbage	Cauliflower
Celery	Chard	Cucumbers	Endive
Radishes	Kohlrabi	Mushrooms	Okra
	Sauerkraut	Zucchini	Yellow Squash

GROUP III: HIGH VITAMIN C FRUITS

One serving of any fruit listed here will meet your daily need for vitamin C.

1 cup of fresh strawberries is 50 calories.

70 calories per serving:

1 cup unsweetened grapefruit sections, (fresh or canned)
6 oz. grapefruit juice
1 medium size orange
6 oz. orange juice
1 cup papaya cubes

GROUP IV: MEDIUM-HIGH VITAMIN C FRUITS

Serve two portions of these each day, or one portion plus one of the starred vegetables listed in Group I. These fruits are 40 calories per serving.

¼ cantaloupe
1 tangerine
½ grapefruit, fresh
1 cup tomato juice
½ cup red raspberries

GROUP V: OTHER FRUITS

1 small apple
2 fresh apricots
½ small banana
½ cup fresh blueberries
2 figs, fresh or dried
½ cup Tokay, Malaga or seedless grapes
1 cup cubed watermelon
⅓ medium papaya
1 small pear
⅓ cup unsweetened pineapple juice
1 Tbsp. seedless raisins
½ cup unsweetened applesauce
Dried apricots, 4 halves
½ cup fresh blackberries
10 dark, sweet cherries
2 dates, fresh or dried
¼ cup grape juice
1 wedge honeydew 7 x 2
½ Mango
1 medium peach
½ cup cubed pineapple
2 medium plums

GROUP VI: MILK

With any diet, a pint of low fat milk a day is a must for adults and this counts as 180 calories. Milk may be incorporated into dishes in the meal or as a beverage with meals or as a snack inbetween meals.

GROUP VII: MEATS

This group includes beef, veal, lamb, pork, ham and poultry, fish, cheese and eggs. We require 375 calories of cooked lean meat or their equivalent every day.

For a 225 calorie serving:

1 slice prime rib roast, 5 x 3½ x ½ in.
1 slice sirloin or round roast, 5 x 4 x ¼ in.
1 slice roast lamb, 4 x 4 x ¼ in.
1 slice baked ham, 5½ x 3½ x ¼ in.
2 slices roast pork, 3 x 1½ x ½ in.
3 slices roast veal, 3 x 2 x ½ in.
1 broiled loin lamb chop
1 broiled pork chop
1 cup low-fat cottage cheese
1 broiled veal chop
1 broiled ground beef patty (4oz. raw)
3 slices roast turkey 3 x 3 x¼ in.
3 slices of roast chicken 3 x 3 x ¼ in.
1 fried breast from 2 lb. chicken
½ cup boned, canned chicken
1 piece broiled halibut, 4 x 3 x ½ in.
1 piece broiled or baked salmon, 4 x 3 x½ in.

For 150 calorie serving:

½ of 2 lb. chicken, broiled
3 medium size chicken livers, broiled
1 piece liver, 3½ x 2½ x ½ in.
2½ slices canned corned beef, 3 x 2¼ x ¼ in.
2 slices bologna
3 slices boiled tongue, 5 x 3 x ⅛ in.
1 frankfurter, boiled
2 slices packaged boiled ham
9 shrimp (20 to the lb.) boiled
12 med. oysters
⅔ cup crab meat
¾ cup low-fat cottage cheese
1 cube cheddar cheese, 1½ in.
2 eggs, boiled or poached
⅓ cup canned salmon
½ cup water packed tuna
1 piece boiled haddock, 4½ x 4 x ½ in.
1 piece boiled mackerel, 4 x 2 x ½ in.
1 fishcake, 2½ in. in diameter
4 small, Atlantic-type sardines
2 large California type sardines
12 cherrystone clams

GROUP VIII: HIGH STARCH FOODS

70 calories without butter or margarine

1 slice bread (16 slices to a lb.)
2 graham crackers
5 square saltines
3 rectangular wafers
½ cup whole wheat cereal
⅓ cup cooked rice
1 small baked or broiled potato
½ medium baked sweet potato
⅓ cup cooked noodles or macaroni
¼ cup baked beans without pork
1 cup popped corn
1 two inch dinner roll
20 oyster crackers
3 square soda crackers
½ cup oatmeal
¾ cup dry cereal flakes or puffs
½ cup cooked grits
½ cup mashed potato (milk added only)
½ cup cooked spaghetti
⅓ cup cooked beans
½ cup corn

GROUP IX: BUTTER, MARGARINE, FATS OR OILS

55 calories per serving

1 pat butter or margarine (1/16 of a stick)
2 Tbsp. light cream
2 Tbsp. dairy sour cream
1 Tbsp. cream cheese
6 small nuts
1½ tsp. vegetable or olive oil
1 Tbsp. heavy cream
1½ tsp. mayo or salad dressing
1 Tbsp. seasoned salad dressing

Quantities to Serve 100 People

COFFEE	- 3 LBS.
LOAF SUGAR	- 3 LBS.
CREAM	- 3 QUARTS
WHIPPING CREAM	- 4 PTS.
MILK	- 6 GALLONS
FRUIT COCKTAIL	- 2½ GALLONS
FRUIT JUICE	- 4 NO. 10 CANS (26 LBS.)
TOMATO JUICE	- 4 NO. 10 CANS (26 LBS.)
SOUP	- 5 GALLONS
OYSTERS	- 18 QUARTS
WEINERS	- 25 LBS.
MEAT LOAF	- 24 LBS.
HAM	- 40 LBS.
BEEF	- 40 LBS.
ROAST PORK	- 40 LBS.
HAMBURGER	- 30-36 LBS.
CHICKEN FOR CHICKEN PIE	- 40 LBS.
POTATOES	- 35 LBS.
SCALLOPED POTATOES	- 5 GALLON
VEGETABLES	- 4 NO. 10 CANS (26 LBS.)
BAKED BEANS	- 5 GALLON
BEETS	- 30 LBS.
CAULIFLOWER	- 18 LBS.
CABBAGE FOR SLAW	- 20 LBS.
CARROTS	- 33 LBS.
BREAD	- 10 LOAVES
ROLLS	- 200
BUTTER	- 3 LBS.
POTATO SALAD	- 12 QUARTS
FRUIT SALAD	- 20 QUARTS
VEGETABLE SALAD	- 20 QUARTS
LETTUCE	- 20 HEADS
SALAD DRESSING	- 3 QUARTS
PIES	- 18
CAKES	- 8
ICE CREAM	- 4 GALLONS
CHEESE	- 3 LBS.
OLIVES	- 1¾ LBS.
PICKLES	- 2 QUARTS
NUTS	- 3 LBS. SORTED

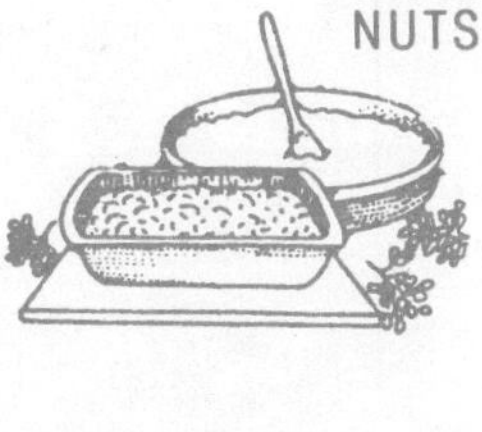

To serve 50 people, divide by 2
To serve 25 people, divide by 4

CALORIES BURNED UP DURING TEN MINUTES OF CONTINUOUS ACTIVITY

According to Body Weight ⇨	Body Wt.#	150#	175#	200#	225#	250#	275#	300#
PERSONAL ACTIVITIES								
Sleeping		12	14	16	18	20	22	24
Sitting (TV or reading)		12	14	16	18	20	22	24
Sitting (Conversing)		18	21	24	28	30	34	37
Washing/Dressing		32	38	42	47	53	58	63
Standing quietly		14	17	19	21	24	26	28
SEDENTARY OCCUPATION								
Sitting/Writing		18	21	24	28	30	34	37
Light Office Work		30	35	39	45	50	55	60
Standing (Light activity)		24	28	32	37	40	45	50
HOUSEWORK								
General Housework		41	48	53	60	68	74	81
Washing Windows		42	49	54	61	69	76	83
Making Beds		39	46	52	58	65	75	85
Mopping Floors		46	54	60	68	75	83	91
Light Gardening		36	42	47	53	59	66	73
Weeding Garden		59	69	78	88	98	109	120
Mowing Grass (power)		41	48	53	60	67	74	81
Mowing Grass (manual)		45	53	58	66	74	81	88
Shoveling Snow		78	92	100	117	130	144	160
LIGHT WORK								
Factory Assembly		24	28	32	37	40	45	50
Truck-Auto Repair		42	49	54	61	69	76	83
Carpentry/Farm Work		38	45	51	58	64	71	78
Brick Laying		34	40	45	51	57	62	67
HEAVY WORK								
Chopping Wood		73	86	96	109	121	134	156
Pick & Shovel Work		67	79	88	100	110	120	130

(# = lb.)

CALORIES BURNED UP DURING TEN MINUTES OF CONTINUOUS ACTIVITY (Continued)

According to Body Weight ⇨	Body Wt.#	150#	175#	200#	225#	250#	275#	300#
LOCOMOTION								
Walking - 2 mph		35	40	46	53	58	64	69
One mile - @ 2 mph		105	120	140	157	175	193	210
Walking - 4½ mph		67	78	87	98	110	120	131
One mile - 4½ mph		89	103	115	130	147	160	173
Walking Upstairs		175	201	229	259	288	318	350
Walking Downstairs		67	78	88	100	111	122	134
Jogging - 5½ mph		108	127	142	160	178	197	215
Running - 7 mph		141	164	187	208	232	256	280
Running - 12 mph (sprint)		197	230	258	295	326	360	395
Running in place (140 count)		242	284	325	363	405	447	490
Bicycle - 5½ mph		50	58	67	75	83	92	101
Bicycle - 13 mph		107	125	142	160	178	197	216
RECREATION								
Badminton or Volleyball		52	67	75	85	94	104	115
Baseball (except pitcher)		47	54	62	70	78	86	94
Basketball		70	82	93	105	117	128	140
Bowling (nonstop)		67	82	90	100	111	122	133
Dancing - moderate		42	49	55	62	69	77	86
Dancing - vigorous		57	67	75	86	94	104	115
Square Dancing		68	80	90	103	113	124	135
Football		83	97	110	123	137	152	167
Golf - foursome		40	47	55	62	68	75	83
Horseback Riding (trot)		67	78	90	102	112	123	134
Ping Pong		38	43	52	58	64	71	78
Skiing - (alpine)		96	113	128	145	160	177	195
Skiing - (cross country)		117	137	158	174	194	214	235
Skiing - (water)		73	92	104	117	130	142	165
Swimming - (backstroke) 20 yd/min		38	43	52	58	64	71	79
Swimming - (breaststroke) 20 yd/min		48	55	63	72	80	88	96
Swimming - crawl 20 yd/min		48	55	63	72	80	88	96
Tennis		67	80	92	103	115	125	135
Wrestling, Judo or Karate		129	150	175	192	213	235	257

(# = lb.)

FIRST AID IN HOUSEHOLD EMERGENCIES

POISONING: When a poison has been taken internally, start first aid at once. Call doctor immediately.

- *Dilute* poison with large amounts of liquids — milk, or water.
- Wash out by inducing vomiting, when not a strong acid, strong alkali or petroleum.
- For acid poisons do not induce vomiting, but neutralize with milk of magnesia. Then give milk, olive oil or egg white. Keep victim warm and lying down.
- For alkali poisons such as lye or ammonia, do not induce vomiting.
- Give lemon juice or vinegar. Then give milk and keep victim warm and lying down.
- If poison is a sleeping drug, induce vomiting and then give strong black coffee frequently. Victim must be kept awake.
- If breathing stops, give artificial respiration.

SHOCK: Shock is brought on by a sudden or severe physical injury or emotional disturbance. In shock, the balance between the nervous system and the blood vessels is upset. The result is faintness, nausea, and a pale and clammy skin. Call ambulance immediately. If not treated the victim may become unconscious and eventually lapse into a coma.

- Keep victim lying down, preferably with head lower than body.
- Don't give fluids unless delayed in getting to doctor, then give only water. (Hot tea, coffee, milk or broth may be tried if water is not tolerated.)
- Never give liquid to an unconscious person. Patient must be alert.
- Cover victim both under and around his body.
- Do not permit victim to become abnormally hot.
- Reassure victim and avoid letting him see other victims, or his own injury.
- Fainting is most common and last form of shock. Patient will respond in 30-60 seconds by merely allowing patient to lie head down if possible on floor.

FRACTURES: Pain, deformity or swelling of injured part usually means a fracture. If fracture is suspected, don't move person unless absolutely necessary, and then only if the suspected area is splinted. Give small amounts of lukewarm fluids and treat for shock.

BURNS: Apply or submerge the burned area in cold water. Apply a protective dry sterile cloth or gauze dry dressing if necessary. Do not apply grease or an antiseptic ointment or spray. Call doctor and keep patient warm (not hot) with severe burns.

- If burn case must be transported any distance, cover burns with clean cloth.
- Don't dress extensive facial burns. (It may hinder early plastic surgery.)

WOUNDS: Minor Cuts—Apply pressure with sterile gauze until bleeding stops. Use antiseptic recommended by your doctor. Bandage with sterile gauze. See your doctor. **Puncture Wounds**—Cover with sterile gauze and consult doctor immediately. Serious infection can arise unless properly treated.

ANIMAL BITES: Wash wounds freely with soap and water. Hold under running tap for several minutes if possible. Apply an antiseptic approved by your doctor and cover with sterile gauze compress. Always see your doctor immediately. So that animal may be held in quarantine, obtain name and address of owner.

HEAT EXHAUSTION: Caused by exposure to heat or sun. Symptoms: Pale face, moist and clammy skin, weak pulse, subnormal temperature, victim usually conscious.

Treatment: Keep victim lying down, legs elevated, victim wrapped in blanket. Give salt water to drink (1 tsp. salt to 1 glass water) ½ glass every 15 minutes. Call doctor.

GENERAL DIRECTIONS FOR FIRST AID

1. Effect a prompt rescue.
2. Maintain an open airway.
3. Control severe bleeding by direct pressure over bleeding site. No tourniquet.
4. Give First Aid for poisoning.
5. Do not move victim unless it is necessary for safety reasons.
6. Protect the victim from unnecessary manipulation and disturbance.
7. Avoid or overcome chilling by using blankets or covers, if available.
8. Determine the injuries or cause for sudden illness.
9. Examine the victim methodically but be guided by the kind of accident or sudden illness and the need of the situation.
10. Carry out the indicated First Aid.

How To Convert To Metric System

Length

When You Know:	Multiply by:	To Find:
millimeters	0.04	inches
centimeters	0.4	inches
meters	3.3	feet
kilometers	0.6	miles
inches	2.54	centimeters
feet	30	centimeters
yards	0.9	meters
miles	1.6	kilometers

Weight

When You Know:	Multiply by:	To Find:
grams	0.035	ounces
kilograms	2.2	pounds
ounces	28	grams
pounds	0.45	kilograms

Volume

When You Know:	Multiply by:	To Find:
milliliters	0.2	teaspoons
milliliters	0.07	tablespoons
milliliters	0.03	fluid ounces
liters	4.23	cups
liters	2.1	pints
liters	1.06	quarts
liters	0.26	gallons
teaspoons	5	milliliters
tablespoons	15	milliliters
fluid ounces	30	milliliters
cups	0.24	liters
pints	0.47	liters
quarts	0.95	liters
gallons	3.8	liters

Temperature

When You Know:	Multiply by:	To Find:
degrees Celsius	9/5, and add 32	degrees Fahrenheit
degrees Fahrenheit	5/9 (after subtracting 32)	degrees Celsius

STEAK COOKING CHART

-To Prepare Your Steaks-

Thaw in refrigerator, bring meat to room temperature before cooking. You can successfully cook frozen steaks. Start by searing both sides to seal in juices. Then reduce heat for slow cooking to allow the inside to thaw. Follow the chart below, but allow about twice the cooking time for frozen steaks.

For juicier and more flavorful steaks, tongs should be used when handling or turning. Cooking units vary of course and it is always advisable to run your own tests when cooking steaks. The chart below is a guide.

The cooking times below are for fully thawed steaks.

Filet Mignons take one to two minutes less total time to cook.

Cooking Instructions		Red-Hot Charcoal 2¾" from heat source		Pre-heated oven broiler 2" from heat source	
Thickness	Doneness	First side	After turning	First side	After turning
¾"	Rare	4 Minutes	2 Minutes	5 Minutes	4 Minutes
	Medium	5 Minutes	3 Minutes	7 Minutes	5 Minutes
	Well	7 Minutes	5 Minutes	10 Minutes	8 Minutes
1"	Rare	5 Minutes	3 Minutes	6 Minutes	5 Minutes
	Medium	6 Minutes	4 Minutes	8 Minutes	6 Minutes
	Well	8 Minutes	6 Minutes	11 Minutes	9 Minutes
1¼"	Rare	5 Minutes	4 Minutes	7 Minutes	5 Minutes
	Medium	7 Minutes	5 Minutes	8 Minutes	7 Minutes
	Well	9 Minutes	7 Minutes	12 Minutes	10 Minutes
1½"	Rare	6 Minutes	4 Minutes	7 Minutes	6 Minutes
	Medium	7 Minutes	6 Minutes	9 Minutes	7 Minutes
	Well	10 Minutes	8 Minutes	13 Minutes	11 Minutes
1¾"	Rare	7 Minutes	5 Minutes	8 Minutes	7 Minutes
	Medium	8 Minutes	7 Minutes	9 Minutes	8 Minutes
	Well	11 Minutes	9 Minutes	14 Minutes	12 Minutes

If you prefer to cook your steaks in your conventional oven, do not thaw, and preheat oven to 450°. As a guide for medium-rare steaks allow approximately:

10-11 minutes per side for an 8 oz. Filet of Prime Rib
12-13 minutes per side for an 8 oz. Top Sirloin
9 minutes per side for an 11 or 12 oz. Boneless Strip Sirloin
10-11 minutes per side for a 6 oz. Filet Mignon

Because ovens may vary in the amount of heat produced and the best distance to place the meat from the burners, tests on your equipment are valuable.

PARENTS' GLOSSARY OF KIDS' KITCHEN TERMS

Appetizing : Anything advertised on TV.
Boil : The point a parent reaches upon hearing the automatic "yuk" before a food is even tasted.
Casserole : Combination of favorite foods that go uneaten because they are mixed together.
Chair : Spot left vacant by mid-meal bathroom visit.
Cookie (Last One) : Item that must be eaten in front of a sibling.
Crust : Part of a sandwich saved for the starving children of: China, India, Africa, or Europe (check one).
Desserts : The reason for eating a meal.
Evaporate : Magic trick performed by children when it comes time to clear the table or wash dishes.
Fat : Microscopic substance detected visually by children on pieces of meat they do not wish to eat.
Floor : Place for all food not found on lap or chair.
Fork : Eating utensil made obsolete by the discovery of fingers.

Fried Foods : Gourmet cooking.
Frozen : Condition of children's jaws when spinach is served.
Fruit : A natural sweet not to be confused with dessert.
Germs : The only thing kids will share freely.
Kitchen : The only room not used when eating crumbly snacks.
Leftovers : Commonly described as "gross".
Liver : A food that affects genes, creating a hereditary dislike.
Lollipop : A snack provided by people who don't have to pay dental bills.
Macaroni : Material for a collage.
Measuring Cup : A kitchen utensil that is stored in the sandbox.
Metric : A system of measurement that will be accepted only after forty years of wandering in the desert.
Napkin : Any worn cloth object, such as shirt or pants.
Natural Food : Food eaten with unwashed hands.
Nutrition : Secret war waged by parents using direct commands, camouflage, and constant guard duty.
Plate : A breakable Frisbee.

Refrigerator : A very expensive and inefficient room air conditioner.
Saliva : A medium for blowing bubbles.
Soda Pop : Shake 'N Spray.
Table : A place for storing gum.
Table Leg : Percussion instrument.
Thirsty : How your child feels after you've said your final "good night".
Vegetable : A basic food known to satisfy kid's hunger - but only by sight.
Water : Popular beverage in underdeveloped countries.

Where to look in the Bible

when

Anxious for dear ones—*Ps. 121; Luke 17.*

Business is poor—*Ps. 37, 92; Eccl. 5.*

Discouraged—*Ps. 23, 42, 43.*

Everything seems going from bad to worse—*II Tim. 3; Heb. 13.*

Friends seem to go back on you—*Matt. 5; I Cor. 13.*

Sorrow overtakes you—*Ps. 46; Matt. 28.*

Tempted to do wrong—*Ps. 15, 19, 139; Matt. 4; James 1.*

Things look "blue"—*Ps. 34, 71; Isa. 40.*

You seem too busy—*Eccl. 3:1-15.*

You can't go to sleep—*Ps. 4, 56, 130.*

You have quarreled—*Matt. 18; Eph. 4; James 4.*

You are weary—*Ps. 95:1-7; Matt. 11.*

Worries oppress you—*Ps. 46; Matt. 6.*

If you

Are challenged by opposing forces—*Eph. 6; Phil. 4.*

Are facing a crisis—*Job 28:12-28; Prov. 8; Isa. 55.*

Are jealous—*Ps. 49; James 3.*

Are impatient—*Ps. 40, 90; Heb. 12.*

Are bereaved—*I Cor. 15; I Thess. 4:13-5:28; Rev. 21, 22.*

Are bored—*II Kings 5; Job 38; Ps. 103, 104; Eph. 3.*

when

Desiring inward peace—*John 14; Rom. 8.*

Everything is going well—*Ps. 33:12-22; 100; I Tim. 6; James 2:1-17.*

Satisfied with yourself—*Prov. 11; Luke 16.*

Seeking the best investment—*Matt. 7.*

Starting a new job—*Ps. 1; Prov. 16; Phil. 3:7-21.*

You have been placed in a position of responsibility—*Joshua 1:1-9; Prov. 2; II Cor. 8:1-15.*

Making a new home—*Ps. 127; Prov. 17; Eph. 5; Col. 3; I Peter 3:1-17; I John 4.*

You are out for a good time—*Matt. 15:1-20; II Cor. 3; Gal. 5.*

Wanting to live successfully with your fellowmen—*Rom. 12.*

to find

The Ten Commandments—*Exo. 20; Deut. 5.*

The Shepherd Psalm—*Ps. 23.*

The Birth of Jesus—*Matt. 1, 2; Luke 2.*

The Beatitudes—*Matt. 5:1-12.*

The Lord's Prayer—*Matt. 6:5-15; Luke 11:1-13.*

The Sermon on the Mount—*Matt. 5, 6, 7.*

The Great Commandments—*Matt. 22:34-40.*

The Great Commission—*Matt. 28:16-20.*

The Parable of the Good Samaritan—*Luke 10.*

The Parable of the Prodigal Son—*Luke 15.*

The Parable of the Sower—*Matt. 13; Mark 4; Luke 8.*

The Last Judgment—*Matt. 25.*

The Crucifixion, Death and Resurrection of Jesus—*Matt. 26, 27, 28; Mark 14, 15, 16; Luke 22, 23, 24; John, Chapters 13 to 21.*

The Outpouring of the Holy Spirit—*Acts 2.*

If you

Bear a grudge—*Luke 6; II Cor. 4; Eph. 4.*

Have experienced severe losses—*Col. 1; I Peter 1.*

Have been disobedient—*Isa. 6; Mark 12; Luke 5.*

Need forgiveness—*Matt. 23; Luke 15; Philemon.*

Are sick or in pain—*Ps. 6, 39, 41, 67; Isa. 26.*

when you

Feel your faith is weak—*Ps. 126, 146; Heb. 11.*

Think God seems far away—*Ps. 25, 125, 138; Luke 10.*

Are leaving home—*Ps. 119; Prov. 3, 4.*

Are planning your budget—*Mark 4; Luke 19.*

Are becoming lax and indifferent—*Matt. 25; Rev. 3.*

Are lonely or fearful—*Ps. 27, 91; Luke 8; I Peter 4.*

Fear death—*John 11, 17, 20; II Cor. 5; I John 3; Rev. 14.*

Have sinned—*Ps. 51; Isa. 53; John 3; I John 1.*

Want to know the way of prayer—*I Kings 8:12-61; Luke 11, 18.*

Want a worshipful mood—*Ps. 24, 84, 116; Isa. 1:10-20; John 4:1-45.*

Are concerned with God in national life—*Deut. 8; Ps. 85, 118, 124; Isa. 41:8-20; Micah 4, 6:6-16.*

courtesy American Bible Society

INDEX OF RECIPES

APPETIZERS, PICKLES AND RELISH

SOUPS, SALADS, DRESSINGS AND SAUCES

MAIN DISHES -
MEAT, SEAFOOD AND POULTRY

MAIN DISHES -
EGG, CHEESE, PASTA AND CASSEROLE

VEGETABLES

BREAD, ROLLS, PIES AND PASTRY

CAKES, COOKIES AND ICINGS

CANDY, JELLY, JAM AND PRESERVES

BEVERAGES AND MISCELLANEOUS

Notes:

Notes:

1990

JANUARY

S	M	T	W	T	F	S
	1	2	3	4	5	6
7	8	9	10	11	12	13
14	15	16	17	18	19	20
21	22	23	24	25	26	27
28	29	30	31			

FEBRUARY

S	M	T	W	T	F	S
				1	2	3
4	5	6	7	8	9	10
11	12	13	14	15	16	17
18	19	20	21	22	23	24
25	26	27	28			

MARCH

S	M	T	W	T	F	S
				1	2	3
4	5	6	7	8	9	10
11	12	13	14	15	16	17
18	19	20	21	22	23	24
25	26	27	28	29	30	31

APRIL

S	M	T	W	T	F	S
1	2	3	4	5	6	7
8	9	10	11	12	13	14
15	16	17	18	19	20	21
22	23	24	25	26	27	28
29	30					

MAY

S	M	T	W	T	F	S
		1	2	3	4	5
6	7	8	9	10	11	12
13	14	15	16	17	18	19
20	21	22	23	24	25	26
27	28	29	30	31		

JUNE

S	M	T	W	T	F	S
					1	2
3	4	5	6	7	8	9
10	11	12	13	14	15	16
17	18	19	20	21	22	23
24	25	26	27	28	29	30

JULY

S	M	T	W	T	F	S
1	2	3	4	5	6	7
8	9	10	11	12	13	14
15	16	17	18	19	20	21
22	23	24	25	26	27	28
29	30	31				

AUGUST

S	M	T	W	T	F	S
			1	2	3	4
5	6	7	8	9	10	11
12	13	14	15	16	17	18
19	20	21	22	23	24	25
26	27	28	29	30	31	

SEPTEMBER

S	M	T	W	T	F	S
						1
2	3	4	5	6	7	8
9	10	11	12	13	14	15
16	17	18	19	20	21	22
23	24	25	26	27	28	29
30						

OCTOBER

S	M	T	W	T	F	S
	1	2	3	4	5	6
7	8	9	10	11	12	13
14	15	16	17	18	19	20
21	22	23	24	25	26	27
28	29	30	31			

NOVEMBER

S	M	T	W	T	F	S
				1	2	3
4	5	6	7	8	9	10
11	12	13	14	15	16	17
18	19	20	21	22	23	24
25	26	27	28	29	30	

DECEMBER

S	M	T	W	T	F	S
						1
2	3	4	5	6	7	8
9	10	11	12	13	14	15
16	17	18	19	20	21	22
23	24	25	26	27	28	29
30	31					

1991

JANUARY

S	M	T	W	T	F	S
		1	2	3	4	5
6	7	8	9	10	11	12
13	14	15	16	17	18	19
20	21	22	23	24	25	26
27	28	29	30	31		

FEBRUARY

S	M	T	W	T	F	S
					1	2
3	4	5	6	7	8	9
10	11	12	13	14	15	16
17	18	19	20	21	22	23
24	25	26	27	28		

MARCH

S	M	T	W	T	F	S
					1	2
3	4	5	6	7	8	9
10	11	12	13	14	15	16
17	18	19	20	21	22	23
24	25	26	27	28	29	30
31						

APRIL

S	M	T	W	T	F	S
	1	2	3	4	5	6
7	8	9	10	11	12	13
14	15	16	17	18	19	20
21	22	23	24	25	26	27
28	29	30				

MAY

S	M	T	W	T	F	S
			1	2	3	4
5	6	7	8	9	10	11
12	13	14	15	16	17	18
19	20	21	22	23	24	25
26	27	28	29	30	31	

JUNE

S	M	T	W	T	F	S
						1
2	3	4	5	6	7	8
9	10	11	12	13	14	15
16	17	18	19	20	21	22
23	24	25	26	27	28	29
30						

JULY

S	M	T	W	T	F	S
	1	2	3	4	5	6
7	8	9	10	11	12	13
14	15	16	17	18	19	20
21	22	23	24	25	26	27
28	29	30	31			

AUGUST

S	M	T	W	T	F	S
				1	2	3
4	5	6	7	8	9	10
11	12	13	14	15	16	17
18	19	20	21	22	23	24
25	26	27	28	29	30	31

SEPTEMBER

S	M	T	W	T	F	S
1	2	3	4	5	6	7
8	9	10	11	12	13	14
15	16	17	18	19	20	21
22	23	24	25	26	27	28
29	30					

OCTOBER

S	M	T	W	T	F	S
		1	2	3	4	5
6	7	8	9	10	11	12
13	14	15	16	17	18	19
20	21	22	23	24	25	26
27	28	29	30	31		

NOVEMBER

S	M	T	W	T	F	S
					1	2
3	4	5	6	7	8	9
10	11	12	13	14	15	16
17	18	19	20	21	22	23
24	25	26	27	28	29	30

DECEMBER

S	M	T	W	T	F	S
1	2	3	4	5	6	7
8	9	10	11	12	13	14
15	16	17	18	19	20	21
22	23	24	25	26	27	28
29	30	31				

1992

JANUARY

S	M	T	W	T	F	S
			1	2	3	4
5	6	7	8	9	10	11
12	13	14	15	16	17	18
19	20	21	22	23	24	25
26	27	28	29	30	31	

FEBRUARY

S	M	T	W	T	F	S
						1
2	3	4	5	6	7	8
9	10	11	12	13	14	15
16	17	18	19	20	21	22
23	24	25	26	27	28	29

MARCH

S	M	T	W	T	F	S
1	2	3	4	5	6	7
8	9	10	11	12	13	14
15	16	17	18	19	20	21
22	23	24	25	26	27	28
29	30	31				

APRIL

S	M	T	W	T	F	S
			1	2	3	4
5	6	7	8	9	10	11
12	13	14	15	16	17	18
19	20	21	22	23	24	25
26	27	28	29	30		

MAY

S	M	T	W	T	F	S
					1	2
3	4	5	6	7	8	9
10	11	12	13	14	15	16
17	18	19	20	21	22	23
24	25	26	27	28	29	30
31						

JUNE

S	M	T	W	T	F	S
	1	2	3	4	5	6
7	8	9	10	11	12	13
14	15	16	17	18	19	20
21	22	23	24	25	26	27
28	29	30				

JULY

S	M	T	W	T	F	S
			1	2	3	4
5	6	7	8	9	10	11
12	13	14	15	16	17	18
19	20	21	22	23	24	25
26	27	28	29	30	31	

AUGUST

S	M	T	W	T	F	S
						1
2	3	4	5	6	7	8
9	10	11	12	13	14	15
16	17	18	19	20	21	22
23	24	25	26	27	28	29
30	31					

SEPTEMBER

S	M	T	W	T	F	S
		1	2	3	4	5
6	7	8	9	10	11	12
13	14	15	16	17	18	19
20	21	22	23	24	25	26
27	28	29	30			

OCTOBER

S	M	T	W	T	F	S
				1	2	3
4	5	6	7	8	9	10
11	12	13	14	15	16	17
18	19	20	21	22	23	24
25	26	27	28	29	30	31

NOVEMBER

S	M	T	W	T	F	S
1	2	3	4	5	6	7
8	9	10	11	12	13	14
15	16	17	18	19	20	21
22	23	24	25	26	27	28
29	30					

DECEMBER

S	M	T	W	T	F	S
		1	2	3	4	5
6	7	8	9	10	11	12
13	14	15	16	17	18	19
20	21	22	23	24	25	26
27	28	29	30	31		

The plastic binding on this book will provide years of endless service, but like all plastic material it should not be exposed to excessive heat. Examples of this would be direct sun, left in a hot automobile or near the burners of a kitchen stove.

DATES TO REMEMBER

	1990	1991	1992
NEW YEAR'S DAY	Monday January 1	Tuesday January 1	Wednesday January 1
DR. KING'S BIRTHDAY	Monday January 15	Monday January 21	Monday January 20
LINCOLN'S BIRTHDAY	Monday February 12	Tuesday February 12	Wednesday February 12
VALENTINE'S DAY	Wednesday February 14	Thursday February 14	Friday February 14
WASHINGTON'S BIRTHDAY (Observed)	Monday February 19	Monday February 18	Monday February 17
ASH WEDNESDAY	Wednesday February 28	Wednesday February 13	Wednesday March 4
ST. PATRICK'S DAY	Saturday March 17	Sunday March 17	Tuesday March 17
PALM SUNDAY	Sunday April 8	Sunday March 24	Sunday April 12
GOOD FRIDAY	Friday April 13	Friday March 29	Friday April 17
EASTER	Sunday April 15	Sunday March 31	Sunday April 19
PASSOVER (First Day)	Tuesday April 10	Saturday March 30	Saturday April 18
MOTHER'S DAY	Sunday May 13	Sunday May 12	Sunday May 10
NATIONAL MEMORIAL DAY (Traditional — Always Observed May 30)	Monday May 28	Monday May 27	Monday May 25
FATHER'S DAY	Sunday June 17	Sunday June 16	Sunday June 21
INDEPENDENCE DAY	Wednesday July 4	Thursday July 4	Saturday July 4
LABOR DAY	Monday September 3	Monday September 2	Monday September 7
ROSH HASHANAH	Thursday September 20	Monday September 9	Monday September 28
YOM KIPPUR	Saturday September 29	Wednesday September 18	Wednesday October 7
COLUMBUS DAY (Observed)	Monday October 8	Monday October 7	Monday October 12
HALLOWEEN	Wednesday October 31	Thursday October 31	Saturday October 31
ELECTION DAY	Tuesday November 6	Tuesday November 5	Tuesday November 3
VETERAN'S DAY	Sunday November 11	Monday November 11	Wednesday November 11
THANKSGIVING	Thursday November 22	Thursday November 28	Thursday November 26
CHANUKAH	Wednesday December 12	Monday December 2	Sunday December 20
CHRISTMAS	Tuesday December 25	Wednesday December 25	Friday December 25